speak

a 9-week small group collision
Obeying the Call

Standard PUBLISHING

Cincinnati, Ohio

CD-ROM with printable
student pages enclosed

speak

Published by Standard Publishing, Cincinnati, Ohio
www.standardpub.com

Copyright © 2010 by CHRIST IN YOUTH

Also available:
Redefining the Win for Jr. High Small Groups, ISBN 978-0-7847-2320-3, copyright © 2010 by CHRIST IN YOUTH
Connect, ISBN 978-0-7847-2405-7, copyright © 2010 by CHRIST IN YOUTH

Printed in: United States of America
Project editors: Kelly Carr, Dana Wilkerson
Cover and interior design: Thinkpen Design, Inc., www.thinkpendesign.com

ISBN 978-0-7847-2406-4

15 14 13 12 11 10   1 2 3 4 5 6 7 8 9

Collision Contents

Your Real Goal

by Johnny Scott

We all want to see life change in teens. Many jr. high youth ministries have discovered the importance of assimilating caring adults into the program who value doing life with adolescents. These ministries have also adopted some form of small group meeting time as a part of their larger vision for ministering to jr. highers. Almost everyone agrees that this small group interaction time can be effective. But after being inundated with the vast amount of curriculum and tools for small group leaders, have you ever found yourself back to square one, asking the question of what to do with jr. high small groups?

The answer is in defining what a great small group meeting looks like. In other words, identify the goal and communicate it to the teens in a way that resonates with them.

Without a new way of defining and communicating the wins during every small group session, many leaders feel like they've failed. Teens get frustrated just like we do, and they pick up on our disappointment with small group time. Some leaders have unrealistic expectations of jr. highers. But the fact is that many teens are not capable of articulating what God is doing in their hearts and minds. Many of these small group experiences are seeds that may not be seen for years. We want adolescents to have that breakthrough.

The act of processing faith issues in an environment with caring adults is a pathway we want to familiarize teens with. This in itself is a major win for a small group. Jr. highers are like wet cement. Very quickly they will be set in their ways. How awesome it is when teens begin to process their thoughts about faith and life in the context of a church small group! That's the payoff, and it can happen!

Constantly redefine the win! Question what you do now, and don't be afraid to experiment with redefining your jr. high small group wins. Here are some win-defining ideas from what others are doing:

- Define the win as one kid finally accepting the hug you have been offering for months.
- Define the win as kids not wanting to leave as soon as the official time is over.
- Define the win as someone remembering *anything* from last week.
- Define the win as pairing caring adults with teens.
- Define the win as trusting the Holy Spirit that more is getting through than meets the eye.
- Define the win as jr. highers simply coming back for more.
- Define the win as knowing adolescents feel loved and not manipulated.
- Define the win as adults being determined to look teens in the eye and simply listen as long as they need to talk. (If you did this at small group, it was a huge win!)
- Define the win as anything that shows you are building a relational bridge with a jr. higher!

Has a kid told you about an event happening in his life this week? It wasn't just conversation. Read between the lines. Are your teens anxious, do they want you to attend their events but don't know how to ask?

Unless they are being forced to attend small group by their parents, jr. highers do have other options. If they decided to come on their own to small group, that's a win.

Did a parent help bring them? That is a win because they feel strongly enough about their involvement to invest the time, gas, and hassle of dropping their teens off and picking them up. That is a huge win you needn't overlook. Did you get the chance to connect with that parent and say thanks? That is a bridge.

Did you get to appropriately touch every kid and say something below the surface level about who they are in God's eyes? If that is *all* you did, the whole evening was a hit! That doesn't happen at school and maybe not even at home.

Did someone bring a friend? That is a big deal if they trust you enough to let you in on their world with their friends.

Did someone express any thought that occurred to them during the week concerning last week's content? That is a huge win, and you must celebrate it. Encourage and praise any teen's attempt to take their faith into other parts of their lives. ✦

For more great strategies, tips, and encouragement, check out Johnny Scott's *Redefining the Win for Jr. High Small Groups*, available from Standard Publishing (ISBN 978-0-7847-2320-3).

Before You Begin

Set list

We've broken each session of this Small Group Collision into sections that can be easily taken apart or rearranged so that you only use the elements and the order that works for your kids and their attention span, maturity, etc.

Collision elements

* **txt a frnd**—teens respond to an icebreaker question by texting each other
* **mic check**—teens play a game or do an activity based on the study's theme
* **solo**—teens read and reflect on Scripture for 5 minutes to prep for the study instead of doing homework before they arrive
* **freestyle**—teens share their reaction to the Scripture or topic by talking or texting
* **strike a chord**—teens study key Scriptures as a group and get into deeper discussion
* **encore**—leader emphasizes key points of the study
* **backstage pass**—teens communicate directly with God through worship, prayer, or contemplation
* **hit the road**—leader wraps up with a focus on life application
* **5 for 5 world tour**—5-minute challenges that teens will do for 5 days each week to put into action what you studied in small group; the leader can send these challenges via text message/e-mail/Facebook/Twitter or print the challenges as a handout from the CD-ROM and send it home with kids

Additional info for the leader

* **hidden track**—helpful tips for the leader about specific activities
* **b4 u meet**—a reminder to send teens before the small group meeting time
* **txt it**—an option in several places during the session allowing teens to text their answers to discussion questions instead of only responding out loud
* **playlist**—songs you may choose to use during your session to relate to the theme
* **aftr u meet**—an encouragement note to send teens after the small group meeting time

Using technology in your small group collision

Text time in the session

Jr. highers love texting. But we don't want them to become distracted by it. So we've come up with a few places in each session where you can allow teens to pull out their cell phones and text the answers to discussion questions to you or to their friends there in small group. Then you can ask them to put their phones away for the remainder of the time. These options allow teens to speak in their communication style within the framework of the small group structure without driving you crazy, we hope! You may choose to use this each session or on occasion.

Music to set the mood

Each session has a playlist of songs that focus on the theme of the study. You may want to download one or more of the songs (or use others you like) to play before, after, or during specific portions of the small group session.

Facebook, Twitter, MySpace

You might want to create your own group on Facebook or start your own Twitter following where all of your jr. highers can join and discuss small group topics during the week. Here you can send reminders to your teens about upcoming sessions and post the **5 for 5 world tour** items (see description on previous page). You could also send these via MySpace, text message, or old school e-mail! :)

1

Great Maker, Great Value

The Prep

Session goal: As jr. highers discover the character of God, they'll begin to better understand their worth as God's creation.

Scriptures: Genesis 1:1–2:3; Job 38–41; Psalm 44:20, 21; Psalm 65:5-7; Psalm 90:2; Psalm 139:8, 13

You'll need:

- ✦ Bibles
- ✦ Pens or pencils
- ✦ Paper
- ✦ 1 or more books with photographs of outer space
- ✦ Ink pad
- ✦ Disposable wipes
- ✦ Garbage can
- ✦ Bowl
- ✦ iPod or CD player
- ✦ CD or MP3 version of "How Great Thou Art" by Passion

Download and print:

- ✦ "Stations" handouts (2 copies of each)
- ✦ **solo/strike a chord** discussion guide (1 per teen)

Optional supplies:

* For **backstage pass:** CD player and CD or iPod with recommended **playlist** songs.
* For **hit the road:** Download and print copies of this week's **5 for 5 world tour** take-home page (1 per teen) if you are unable to use the technology options.

Setting it up:

* You will need to make 2 sets of 6 famous paintings. At the top of each piece of paper, write the name of the painting (but not the artist). Then do a Web search for an image of the painting, print it out, and tape it to the paper. Use the following 6 paintings:

    Portrait of Adele Bloch-Bauer I by Gustav Klimt
    Portrait of Dr. Gachet by Vincent van Gogh
    Bal au moulin de la Galette by Pierre-Auguste Renoir
    Garçon à la pipe by Pablo Picasso
    Dora Maar au Chat by Pablo Picasso
    Irises by Vincent van Gogh

* Set up 4 Experience Stations as follows:

    Station 1: Set out 2 copies of the handout, several Bibles, and 1 or more books with photographs of outer space. (Option: Set this station up outside so kids can look at the sun or at the moon and stars.)

    Station 2: Set out 2 copies of the handout, several Bibles, an ink pad, disposable wipes, a piece of paper, and a garbage can.

    Station 3: Set out 2 copies of the handout and several Bibles.

    Station 4: Set out 2 copies of the handout, several Bibles, and pens or pencils.

- Print out the text of Job 38–41 from www.biblegateway.com or photocopy it from your own Bible. Cut out verses or sections that draw attention to God's awesomeness as Creator; you'll want at least 1 verse per teen. Fold the slips you've cut out and put them in a bowl.
- If you'd like to use the optional **playlist** recommendations, download songs of your choice from *Bach: The Cello Suites* by Yo-Yo Ma and from *City On a Hill: Sing Alleluia* by various artists and ready your iPod or burn a CD in order to play the songs during the session.

Leader insight:

What is God like? This is a question that philosophers and theologians have pondered through the ages. From a biblical perspective, how we answer this question has a far-reaching implication as to how we view the world. What this session will explore is another often-overlooked implication: what God's characteristics reveal about *ourselves*.

Imagine for a moment the perspective of a person who believes there's no god designing, crafting, or at work behind the scenes. According to this mind-set, there's no basis whatsoever for human dignity. We are little more than animals, and any sense of human value is merely a social construct.

But to affirm that God created us says something profound; it asserts that we have value. Like great works of art, our value is derived from the greatness of our maker. If our maker is God Almighty, then our value is inestimable.

You may have already spent time teaching your teens about what God is like. If they've grown up in the church, they've probably heard these concepts before—but they're well worth pondering again and again. Truths like "God is all knowing" or "God is all powerful" shouldn't be phrases that we toss around and take for granted. When we take the time to really chew on these realities, we're brought to our knees in awe. We get a sense of how great God is, how small we are, and yet, ironically, how significant we are in God's eyes.

Your teens are at a critical time in their lives. They are experiencing tremendous amounts of self-doubt. Even the seemingly confident kids in your group are inwardly struggling with concerns about their shortcomings, confusion about their identities, loneliness, and the heavy burden of everybody else's opinion of them. As you draw them into a collision with how totally amazing God is, they'll begin to get a sense of the *value* they have in God's eyes. They are masterpieces of the artist who crafted the universe!

So what about you? You've read the books, heard (or perhaps preached) the sermons, and can easily recite the most important characteristics of God. So have they become old hat to *you*? Are you calloused to the wonder they should draw forth in your soul? When was the last time you really pondered God's awe-inspiring nature and what it says about your place in this universe?

As you prepare to lead (and join) your teens in this adventure, pray:

God, you are great. And God, I so often lose sight of your greatness. I worship you as the maker of all things. You are the source of true meaning and value in my life. Please help me to communicate who you are to my jr. highers—and please reveal yourself to them in powerful ways. In Jesus' name, amen.

b4 u meet

A couple of days before your group meets, send a text message to your kids letting them know how excited you are to begin this Speak study with them. (If some teens don't text, send them an e-mail or a message on Facebook or MySpace.)

The Session

Rearrange or delete sections of the study to best meet your group's needs.

txt a frnd about 5 minutes

Invite your small group to consider this question:

✦ In your opinion, what's one of the coolest things God has made? Why do you think that?

When they've got an answer, invite them to get out their cell phones and text their answer to another person in the room. (If kids don't have their own phone, they could borrow a friend's or could form pairs and talk about their answer to this question.)

When you're ready to move on to the next part of the study, have them put their cell phones away for now. ✦

mic check about 8 minutes

Divide the kids into 2 teams. Place 1 set of the 6 paintings on the floor by each group, in mixed-up order. Tell kids that these are 6 of the most expensive paintings in the world. Challenge them to put the paintings in order of most expensive to least expensive. Give them 2 minutes to do this. When you reveal the answers, also tell kids the artist and estimated value of each painting.

Answer Key (from www.renoirgallery.com):

1. *Portrait of Adele Bloch-Bauer I* by Gustav Klimt ($135 million)
2. *Portrait of Dr. Gachet* by Vincent van Gogh ($117 million)
3. *Bal au moulin de la Galette* by Pierre-Auguste Renoir ($110 million)

4. *Garçon à la pipe* by Pablo Picasso ($107 million)
5. *Dora Maar au Chat* by Pablo Picasso ($95 million)
6. *Irises* by Vincent van Gogh ($78 million)

Then say: You may have noticed that the most famous painting in the world—the Mona Lisa by Leonardo Da Vinci—wasn't included. That's because it is considered to be so treasured that its value cannot be adequately conveyed by a price tag.

Ask the group:

✦ When you were putting the paintings in order, what were the most important factors in determining how you ranked the paintings?

Explain that several factors go into determining the value of a painting: its history or circumstances, age, subject, and actual beauty are all important. But perhaps the most important factor for determining worth is the artist.

Share with your teens how as Christians we believe in an all-powerful, all-knowing, and ever-present being called God. By way of analogy, say: If we think of God as an artist and we are his creation, then our worth is linked to God himself. How we think of God tells us something about us.

Ask kids:

✦ Is there a being greater than God? Is it even possible to think hypothetically of a being that's greater than God? Why or why not?

After a bit of silence (or talking if the kids choose to engage verbally with this question), continue by saying: Think about what this means. If God is the ultimate artist and we are his masterpiece, his greatest work of art, then this means that we are inherently of great value. When we read the creation account in the Bible, we can see that humans are set apart as something very special. ✦

solo/strike a chord handout

solo `about 5 minutes`

Tell your kids you'd like them to find a spot in your meeting area where they can be alone and spend about 5 minutes reading Scripture and thinking about what it means.

Give each teen a copy of the **solo/strike a chord** handout and a pen or pencil, inviting them to read and follow the instructions. (Have them read through only the top portion, **solo**, right now and they'll need the **strike a chord** portion in a few minutes.) Here's a copy of what they'll read:

Take 5 minutes to read Genesis 1:1–2:3.

Consider:
* What do you observe in this passage?
* What stands out to you most about God in this passage? Why is this important to you?

When the kids understand what they're supposed to do, have them take off and find a spot to read and reflect. After about 5 minutes, call everybody back together. ✦

Station 1 handout

freestyle `about 20 minutes`

Tell kids that they're going to have an opportunity to spend some time discovering more about what God is like. Let them know that you've set up 4 stations in your meeting area, and point out where each of them is located. (Depending on how you've set things up, Station 1 may be outside.) Let kids know that they'll find instructions at each station for something to read, something to think about, and something to do. Explain that they'll have about 5 minutes per station, so they should take their time to really think about each characteristic of God they learn about. Kids can move at their own individual pace. Though they should aim to visit all of the stations, it's fine if they don't get through all of them.

Make sure everyone understands your directions. Divide the kids among the stations, and have everyone get started. As kids visit the various stations, keep track of the time. Let them know when 10 minutes are left and when 5 minutes are left. ✤

strike a chord ▸ about 7 minutes

To help kids debrief the experience stations and take another look at today's Scripture passages, have them look at the bottom portion of the **solo/strike a chord** handout. Use it to guide your small group Bible exploration and discussion together as a group. Here's a copy of the **strike a chord** text for you to use to guide your discussion time:

Summarize Genesis 1:1–2:3, and reread Psalm 44:20, 21; Psalm 65:5-7; Psalm 90:2; Psalm 139:8; and Psalm 139:13 together and talk about these questions:

playlist

To add a contemplative ambiance to this experience, download these songs to your iPod (or to a CD) and play them while teens explore the stations:
Songs of your choice from Bach: The Cello Suites by Yo-Yo Ma
Songs of your choice from City On a Hill: Sing Alleluia by various artists

solo/strike a chord handout

txt it

If you want, invite kids to answer these questions both by talking aloud and by texting. As some share their answers, others can text them to you. Read some of their thoughts aloud and build upon their ideas as your group explores this topic together.

✦ What are your thoughts about God now that you know more about the vast universe that he spoke into existence?

✦ God knows you better than you even know yourself. He took great care and gave much attention to creating you. How does this help you appreciate God even more?

✦ When you think about the awesome power of hurricanes, tornadoes, volcanoes, and earthquakes, and that God's authority extends far beyond these natural forces, what is your emotional response to God? Is it fear? Trust? Awe? Explain.

✦ How do these ideas change the way you view yourself or your relationship with God? What does this mean for the way you think about prayer? ✦

encore [about 5 minutes]

Say: We find our worth in who our maker is and what our maker is like. Invite the group to brainstorm with you, sharing their thoughts and ideas about humanity in light of what they have discovered about God today. Encourage kids to say whatever comes to their minds, even if it may initially sound strange. For example, one jr. higher may say, "We seem so small and insignificant because of the how huge the universe is." On the other hand, another teen may say the opposite, "We are really important to God because he made this whole, awesome universe for us to live in." Both of these responses are true. Affirm teens as they share their observations.

Then say: We may feel small when we truly consider how huge our universe is or how powerful great earthquakes and hurricanes are. When we think about how amazing God is, it does make us realize how very, very tiny and powerless we are. This feeling of smallness is appropriate and healthy because it really helps us to have perspective on ourselves and how limited we are. It sort of puts us in our place.

But there is also a certain dignity that we should feel when we really think about the truth that we were created by this all-powerful God. When we think about ourselves, so often we think about all the things we don't like. But, when we think of ourselves, we should think first about our great and good creator. We were each made by the amazing, awesome, loving, powerful, almighty God. Our dignity and worth are connected with our creator's goodness and greatness. We were each made by the greatest artist of all time; that makes each of us more valuable than we can ever truly understand. 🌟

backstage pass about 5 minutes

On a CD player or iPod, play "How Great Thou Art" by Passion. Explain to kids that while the music plays, you'd like them to listen to the words and thank God for his wonderful creation. 🌟

hit the road about 5 minutes

Tell the group you're going to read some Scripture passages together. Set out the bowl of verses from Job 38–41. Invite kids to come up one by one and select a paper, then read it aloud.

When the verses have been read, say: We cannot see the wind, but we see its power as we watch leaves move or tree branches bend. In the same way, we may not be able to see God, but we can see his power and authority displayed all over the world in countless ways. And when we see what God has created, we can be reminded of our great worth as part of that creation.

aftr u meet

Right after your meeting, send kids the first **5 for 5 world tour** challenge for them to do tomorrow via Twitter, e-mail, or by posting it on a Facebook page (or youth group Web page) you've set up. Continue to send 1 challenge each day for the 5 days following your meeting.

About 2 days after your group meets, send a text message to your kids, encouraging them to think about their great worth as God's creation. Prompt them to keep at it with their **5 for 5 world tour** challenges and let them know you're praying for them.

Let your kids know you'll be sending **5 for 5 world tour** life application and devotional challenges for them to do each day via Twitter, e-mail, or through a Facebook group you've set up. (Or, if you prefer not to use these technology options, pass out copies of the **5 for 5 world tour** handout you've downloaded from the CD-ROM to the teens.) Encourage your kids to strive to spend about 5 minutes each day connecting with God through these devotional experiences.

5 for 5 world tour handout

2

Marked with His Image

The Prep

Session goal: Jr. highers will discover the implications of being made in God's image: being "like" him, belonging to him, and being created for a relationship with him.

Scriptures: Genesis 1:24-31; Matthew 22:15-21; John 14:8-11

You'll need:

* Bibles
* Pens or pencils
* Paper
* 3 7-foot lengths of roll paper
* 3 rubber bands
* Washable markers
* Scissors
* 1 10-foot length of roll paper

* 3 pennies
* 3 nickels
* 3 dimes
* 3 quarters
* 3 half-dollars
* 3 resealable plastic bags
* Play paper money (1 bill per kid)

Download and print:

* "Quotes" handout (1 copy)
* "Prayer" handout (1 per kid)
* **solo/strike a chord** discussion guide (1 per kid)

Optional supplies:

✦ For **backstage pass:** CD player and CD or iPod with recommended **playlist** songs.
✦ For **hit the road:** Download and print copies of this week's **5 for 5 world tour** take-home page (1 per teen) if you are unable to use the technology options.

Setting it up:

✦ Put 1 of each coin into each of the resealable plastic bags.
✦ If you'd like to use the optional **playlist** recommendations, download the songs "Meant to Live" and "The Beautiful Letdown" by Switchfoot and ready your iPod or burn a CD in order to play the songs during the session.

Leader insight:

You are special. You are unique. You are meant for something amazing. These statements can sound overused and cheesy, especially when they're parroted over and over again by jr. high guidance counselors. But they're true. We're made in God's image—and exploring this miraculous truth is much more than an exercise in self-esteem.

In this session, you'll lead teens into an examination of what it means (and what it *doesn't* mean) to be made in the image of God. You'll need to carefully navigate this mystery with your kids and help them avoid some common misunderstandings.

First, affirming that we are made "like God" is *not* the same as the New Age philosophies that assert that we are godlike or are divine ourselves. We are sinful, fallen humans. But for this study, you'll be exploring our kingly nature—we're made in the image of the King of kings. He is always God, and we are always beneath him; we are not equals to God, nor will we ever be. But he did give us a royal dignity in his likeness. C.S. Lewis represented this concept well in *The Lion, the Witch and the Wardrobe* and *Prince Caspian*. In both of these books, Aslan is clearly the ultimate king over Narnia, far and away seen as the most powerful, respected, and esteemed being. Yet he places the Pevensie children on the thrones to serve as kings and queens. They are destined and set apart for this royal position in Narnia, but they are never equivalent to Aslan. If your jr. highers are into the Narnia stories, you may want to share this illustration with them.

Second, being made in God's image does not have to do with our abilities or external traits. God's image is reflected in the nature of the human soul, and this image is imprinted on *every* human being, from a tiny unborn embryo to an infirm and crippled elderly person. Though we may reflect traits of God—such as love, creativity, intellect, and so on—be sure to clarify for your teens that even human beings who are unable to do any of those things due to disabilities or other limitations are still made in God's image. When people erroneously tie their understanding of God's image with human abilities, the value of human life begins to erode.

Being made in God's image is both a wonderful and difficult part of the human experience, and this study will explore both sides of the coin. The wonderful part is the value, dignity, and true esteem we begin to feel as we realize this extraordinary truth about ourselves. But there are difficulties too—writers like Augustine, Pascal, Chesterton, Lewis, and many others have zeroed in on the sense of longing and emptiness that accompanies living in this world when we're made for another. Lewis touches on this again in the beginning of *Prince Caspian* as he portrays the difficulty the Pevensie children had living back in England after having ruled as kings and queens. Deep inside they knew they were Narnian royalty, yet in England they were just like everybody else. It was a difficult adjustment and mirrors our human experience on Earth.

As you prepare for this study, pray: God, help me understand more about what it means that I am made in your image. Help me communicate to my teens that each and every one of them is made in your image. Allow us to get just a glimpse of what this mystery means. Help us to begin to live in a way that better reflects your image to the world around us. In Jesus' name, amen.

b4 u meet

A couple of days before your group meets, send a text message to your kids reminding them of the upcoming Speak study. (If some teens don't text, send them an e-mail or a message on Facebook or MySpace.)

The Session

Rearrange or delete sections of the study to best meet your group's needs.

txt a frnd [about 5 minutes]

Invite your small group to consider this question:

❋ Which of your family members do you most look or act like? What similar characteristics do you have?

When they've got an answer, invite them to get out their cell phones and text their answer to another person in the room. (If kids don't have their own phone, they could borrow a friend's or could form pairs and talk about their answer to this question.)

When you're ready to move on to the next part of the study, have them put their cell phones away for now. ❋

mic check [about 8 minutes]

Separate kids into 3 groups. Explain that in a moment you'll be sending the groups off to their own area where they'll have just 5 minutes to complete a challenge: Create a paper "copy" of 1 of their group members. They will need to trace a team member's outline, cut out the outline, and color their copy to look as much like the real person as possible: hair, face, clothing, shoes, jewelry, etc. When 5 minutes are up, teams will roll up their paper copies, put a rubber band around them, and bring them to you. They should keep the identity of who they copied a secret.

Direct teams to different areas where they cannot be easily seen by the other groups (you may want to use a hallway or another empty room). When teams are ready, tell them to begin.

When time is up, collect their rolled up copies and mix them up. Then unroll the copies one by one, inviting kids to guess who they think it's supposed to be. Then invite the group to help you determine which copy is most like the real person. Have the kids vote by cheering, then select which one you think got the loudest cheers and declare it the winner. Congratulate all of the kids on a job well done. ❧

solo `about 5 minutes`

solo/strike a chord handout

Tell your kids you'd like them to find a spot in your meeting area where they can be alone and spend about 5 minutes reading Scripture and thinking about what it means.

Explain that they'll be looking again at a passage they studied last week. In the previous study, they focused on what the passage revealed about God as creator, but this time they'll be zeroing in on the created beings.

Give each teen a copy of the **solo/strike a chord** handout and a pen or pencil, inviting them to read and follow the instructions. (Have them read through only the top portion, **solo**, right now and they'll need the **strike a chord** portion in a few minutes.) Here's a copy of what they'll read:

Take 5 minutes to read Genesis 1:24-31. Consider:

❧ What do you think this passage means?

❧ What stands out to you most from this passage? Why?

When the kids understand what they're supposed to do, have them take off and find a spot to read and reflect. After about 5 minutes, call everybody back together. ✦

solo/strike a chord handout

strike a chord　about 8 minutes

Have the group now look at the bottom portion of the **solo/strike a chord** handout and use it to guide your small group Bible exploration and discussion together as a group. Here's a copy of the **strike a chord** text for you to use to guide your discussion time:

Read Genesis 1:24-31 with a partner. Then consider how it compares or contrasts to the rest of Genesis 1 and answer the following question:

✦ What are 4 things you learn about humankind from this section of the creation account?

After a few minutes, ask pairs to share their ideas. Then share some of your observations about humankind from Genesis 1:24-31. You may want to point out the following:

✦ God creates man in his image.
✦ Man holds a position of authority on earth.
✦ Humans are the only species about which the account specifies "male and female."
✦ God uniquely blesses them.
✦ They are told to "fill" the earth.
✦ God finally determines that his work is *very* good after his creation of humanity. ✦

freestyle [about 12 minutes]

Explain that you're going to explore what it means to be made in the image of God. Read Millard Erickson's quote from the "Quotes" handout aloud twice. Then ask these questions, inviting anyone to share their thoughts:

❤ What is Erickson saying here? How would you put this idea into your own words?

❤ Why do you think he says the image of God isn't about something people have or something people do?

❤ How do you think you would explain what it means to be made in the image of God?

Then share how you'd summarize Erickson's idea in your own words.

Tell kids that in most ancient religions, people believed that they were created to be slaves to the gods. The Bible, on the other hand, presents a uniquely high view of humanity, especially in contrast with other ancient religions. The Bible claims that though we are fallen and sinful, God has given us something special. There is something extraordinary about humanity that sets us apart from all the other living things God made. It is not just that we are full of dignity because we're made by God, but it's that we are something very special and precious—we are *like* God.

Explain that obviously there are a lot of ways we *aren't* like God. For example, we aren't all-powerful or all-knowing. Furthermore, we're sinners, and that sin screws up a lot of things in our lives and in this world.

txt it

You may want to give your teens the option of texting their answers to these questions to you during your discussion time. Read some of their answers out loud and use them as springboards for further discussion.

Quotes handout

Then ask: ?

✦ What are some of the ways we are like God—ways we reflect a bit
of what God is like?

Say: God did not create us to serve him as slaves. After all, God isn't a
slave—he's the King of kings! So if we are made in his image, that means he's
set us apart from all creation to be kingly, to be like him. Deep in our souls
he has given us a sense of nobility. There's a sense that we were made for
something special, for something more. Along with the dignity of being made in
his image, God gave us the honor of having a relationship with him.

Read the first quote from Blaise Pascal's *Pensées* and let kids think
about it for a moment. You may need to reread it a couple of times.
Explain that what Pascal is saying here is that people were made by
God and in his image. We were meant to enjoy his presence, but
because of sin, we are a fallen people—kicked out of the garden
and separated from that relationship. We're like a king who's been
shamed and kicked off his throne. We're like royalty living the lives of
peasants. We have a sense that we're meant for so much more.

Tell kids that the gist of what Pascal is saying is that we will never
be happy unless we are back in relationship with God. Humanity
is special in this regard. Then read the second quote from Pascal in
order to drive home the point. ✦

backstage pass `about 10 minutes`

Invite kids to think about creative ways they could explain what
it means to be made in the image of God, but to also be a sinful
person here on earth. Share this example to help them start thinking.
Say: The image of God is like being a beautiful, expensive, and important painting by Michelangelo that's stuck in somebody's dirty, smelly
basement rather than on display at a museum.

Encourage them to think creatively and to try to come up with analogies for the concept of being made in the image of God using nature, history, art, literature, music, human relationships, or science. Invite them to gather around the piece of roll paper you've placed on the floor and use markers to write their metaphors and analogies or to draw pictures or symbols that convey the idea of what being made in the image of God means to them.

After about 6 minutes for writing and drawing, prompt kids to step back and look at the mural, observing what others have added to it. Ask:

✦ What ideas or images on this mural stand out to you? Why? ✦

encore   about 8 minutes

Divide kids into 3 teams and give each team a bag of coins, a piece of paper, and a pencil. Challenge them to try to identify the name of the person whose image is on each coin.

After about 2 minutes, have kids call out their answers and reveal the correct ones. Then have kids give back the bags of coins.

Answer Key:

Penny = Abraham Lincoln
Nickel = Thomas Jefferson
Dime = Franklin Delano Roosevelt
Quarter = George Washington
Half-dollar = John F. Kennedy

playlist

To add some powerful ambiance to this meditative experience, download these songs to your iPod (or to a CD) and play them (in this order) while teens work. Encourage them to listen to the words as well.
"Meant to Live" by Switchfoot
"The Beautiful Letdown" by Switchfoot

Then have everyone turn to Matthew 22:15-21 in their Bibles. Ask volunteers to read the passage aloud while everyone else follows along in their own Bibles.

Say: I want us to think for a minute about what Jesus meant when he said, "Give to Caesar what belongs to Caesar, and give to God what belongs to God" (Matthew 22:21). Give everyone a piece of play money. Have them each write "Give to God what belongs to God" on their bill.

Explain that in this passage, the Pharisees are trying to get Jesus to say something that might get him in trouble. So Jesus asked the Pharisees for a coin. (Hold up 1 of the larger coins from 1 of the bags.) Then Jesus asked them whose picture was on the coin. In the Greek language this word is *eikon* (pronounced A-cone)—it literally means *image*. Jesus was saying to them, "Whose *image* is this?"

Say: You see, the point is both simple and powerful: Give to your earthly rulers the menial things like money for taxes. Money is marked with their image, after all, so it belongs to them. But we're supposed to give to God what belongs to him. Like a coin, you bear God's image. You belong to God. You are marked forever with his likeness. So what does it mean for us to give to God what belongs to him? It means we give ourselves to him.

Invite kids to close their eyes and prayerfully think about some questions. Each time you ask the question, emphasize a different part in it (see italics). Ask:

* What does it *mean* to you to be created by God?
* What does it mean to *you* to be created by God?
* What does it mean to you to be *created* by God?
* What does it mean to you to be created by *God?*
* What does it mean to you to be created by God *in his image?*

hit the road `about 4 minutes`

Get everyone's attention and say: **You are made in God's image. You belong to him. You belong in a relationship with him. Fold up your fake dollar bill and put it in your purse or wallet to remind you that you are marked with God's image.**

Give everyone a "Prayer" handout; on the handout is the text of a prayer by St. Augustine. Invite the group to pray it aloud together.

Let your kids know you'll be sending **5 for 5 world tour** life application and devotional challenges for them to do each day via Twitter, e-mail, or through a Facebook group you've set up. (Or, if you prefer not to use these technology options, pass out copies of the **5 for 5 world tour** handout you've downloaded from the CD-ROM to the teens.) Encourage your kids to strive to spend about 5 minutes each day connecting with God through these devotional experiences. 🔸

Prayer handout

5 for 5 world tour handout

aftr u meet

Right after your meeting, send kids the first **5 for 5 world tour** challenge for them to do tomorrow via Twitter, e-mail, or by posting it on a Facebook page (or youth group Web page) you've set up. Continue to send 1 challenge each day for the 5 days following your meeting.

About 2 days after your group meets, send a text message to your kids, encouraging them to remember they're created in the image of God. Prompt them to keep at it with their **5 for 5 world tour** challenges and let them know you're praying for them.

My New Life

The Prep

Session goal: Jr. highers will look at the idea of salvation not only as being saved from Hell in the future, but as being saved *now,* in the present, as we discover and live the new life God has called us to.

Scriptures: John 3:3-8; John 4:13, 14; John 6:28-35; John 7:37, 38; John 8:12; Romans 6:23; 2 Corinthians 5:17; Ephesians 4:17-24; Hebrews 1:2, 3

You'll need:

- Bibles
- Pens or pencils
- 2 or more Hula Hoop® rings
- White index cards
- Multicolored index cards
- Roll of black masking tape (the kind you can use on your walls)
- Roll of white masking tape
- Roll of blue masking tape
- Pitcher of water
- Cups (1 per teen)
- Loaf of bread
- Candle
- Matches

Download and print:

- "Word Pictures" handout (1 per every 2 kids)
- **solo/strike a chord** discussion guide (1 per teen)

Optional supplies:

- For **backstage pass:** CD player and CD or iPod with recommended **playlist** songs.
- For **hit the road:** Download and print copies of this week's **5 for 5 world tour** take-home page (1 per teen) if you are unable to use the technology options.

Setting it up:

- If you'd like to use the optional **playlist** recommendations, download the songs "Light (Remix)" and "Captivated (Remix)" by Shawn McDonald and ready your iPod or burn a CD in order to play the songs during the session.

Leader insight:

"If you were killed in a car accident tonight, do you know for certain you'd go to Heaven?"

Sometimes questions like these are strong-arm tactics used by high-pressure evangelists to win souls, but other times they're asked with love and compassion from a well-meaning person who's trying to get a friend to really consider their eternal destiny. In an effort to challenge your jr. highers, you may have asked them this question or one like it. And it's a really good question—a matter we should all consider with seriousness—but it only tells *part* of the story.

This question naturally leads into a presentation of the gospel that's focused on eternal life after death. It zeroes in on avoiding the punishment of Hell. Its emphasis is on the distant future, not the here and now.

Jesus spent an awful lot of his time talking about the here and now—challenging his followers to live differently, inviting them into a process of regeneration that begins in this earthly life, calling his listeners to a full, satisfying, abundant life right here in the flesh. A full-pictured reading of the New Testament's teaching on salvation shows us not something that starts or happens at death, but a process that begins the very moment a person chooses to follow Christ as Savior and Lord and is completed (or fully realized) when we die and go to Heaven.

In this study, you'll transition from the last 2 weeks' focus on God as the creator, to the God who is still at work creating and recreating *even now* through the process of salvation in human lives. You'll help kids see that not only are they saved the moment they accept Jesus as Savior, but they are also in the process of *being saved* throughout their lives as God works in them, drawing them toward spiritual maturity and a vibrant Christian life.

As you prepare to teach this session, don't just think about these things in light of your jr. highers, think also about your own spiritual life. Are you living an abundant, full, and vibrant life? Are you finding satisfaction, meaning, nourishment, and purpose in your relationship with Christ? Or have you slipped into habits of taking your faith for granted? Prayerfully consider how God may be speaking to you through these same Scripture passages about the work he is doing in your life.

In preparation for leading this small group session, pray: Bread of life, help me always seek to find my sustenance for living in you and you alone. Living water, refresh and renew and cleanse me. Light of life, show me the pathway of your truth in this dark world. Jesus, you are the resurrection and the life. Help me adequately communicate this to the teens you've entrusted into my care, and continue to speak to me in my own heart about your work in my life, creating me anew. You are the light of my life. Amen.

b4 u meet

A couple of days before your group meets, send a text message to your kids asking them to think about what salvation means. (If some teens don't text, send them an e-mail or a message on Facebook or MySpace.)

The Session

Rearrange or delete sections of the study to best meet your group's needs.

txt a frnd `about 5 minutes`

Invite your small group to consider this question:

✤ What do you think it means to be saved?

When they've got an answer, invite them to get out their cell phones and text their answer to another person in the room. (If kids don't have their own phone, they could borrow a friend's or could form pairs and talk about their answer to this question.)

When you're ready to move on to the next part of the study, have them put their cell phones away for now. ✤

mic check `about 7 minutes`

Open the session with a contest using Hula Hoop® rings. Hand out as many rings as you have. First, have kids get the rings going around their waists and see who can go the longest without the ring dropping. Next, challenge them to see who can rotate a ring the fastest. Then, see if anyone can spin more than 1 ring at a time. Make sure each kid tries at least 1 of the challenges.

When you're done, have everyone gather back in the center of the room. Say: An ancient Christian thinker named Aquinas attempted to prove the existence of God through the analogy of motion. He basically said that if an object is moving we can safely assume it had a cause and a causer. In other words, those rings didn't just start twirling around your bodies on their own. Someone began the movement. According to Aquinas, the same could be said of the world. The world must have had a beginning, and it must have been set into motion by God.

Aquinas has as many defenders as critics of his argument. I'm not sharing this with you so we can discuss whether or not God created the world—we've already studied the truth of his creation over the past 2 weeks. But I bring this up because Aquinas's idea can help us understand something else: that God not only began the universe, but he's actively involved in continuing its existence.

freestyle `about 5 minutes`

Ask a kid to twirl 1 of the rings around his or her hips for a few seconds, and then instruct the volunteer to stop and let the ring fall. Say: Did God create the world—get things going—and then just stop creating or being involved? No, God is very active and interested in the world today.

Read Hebrews 1:2, 3 aloud. Explain that God created the universe "through the Son." And now, Jesus sustains the created world by his Word.

Read 2 Corinthians 5:17 aloud. Ask:

❋ What do you observe in this verse? What stands out to you?

Encourage kids to share their initial observations, even if they are obvious things. Affirm and summarize kids' input, then say: God is described as creating humanity in the spiritual sense here. God is creating anew—he is creating again.

txt it

You may want to give your teens the option of texting their answers to questions to you during your discussion time. Read some of their answers out loud and use them as springboards for further discussion.

solo/strike a chord handout

solo about 5 minutes

Tell your kids you'd like them to find a spot in your meeting area where they can be alone and spend about 5 minutes reading Scripture and thinking about what it means. Remind them that last week they read about being made in God's image and being created for a relationship with him. Now they'll read about living the new life God has called them to.

Give each teen a copy of the **solo** handout and a pen or pencil, inviting them to read and follow the instructions. (Have them read through only the top portion, **solo**, right now and they'll need the **strike a chord** portion in a few minutes.) Here's a copy of what they'll read:

Take 5 minutes to read Ephesians 4:17-24 and John 3:3-8. Consider:
✤ What do you think these passages mean?
✤ What stands out to you most from these passages? Why?

When the kids understand what they're supposed to do, have them take off and find a spot to read and reflect. After about 5 minutes, call everybody back together. ✤

strike a chord about 15 minutes

Have teens look at the bottom of the **solo/strike a chord** handout and use it to guide your Bible exploration and discussion together as a group. Here's a copy of the **strike a chord** text for you to use to guide your discussion time:

Reread Ephesians 4:17-24 and John 3:3-8 and discuss the following:

✤ What does the image of clothing—of "throwing off" an old way of life and "putting on" a new one—communicate about what it means to be saved? How does it help you understand what salvation means?

✤ How about the idea of being "born again"? What does this word picture communicate to you about what salvation means?

Make sure each teen has a white index card and a pen or pencil. Tell kids you'll be discussing the answers as a group, but also ask them to write their own thoughts about these questions on their index cards. They should hold onto these cards to use in a few minutes.

Explain that you're going to use tape to represent the time line of a person's life. Ask 1 kid to start at the far left side of the wall and stick the end of the black tape to the wall about waist high. Another kid should then roll the tape about $^2/_3$ of the way across the wall and tear it off.

Tell kids that the left end of the line represents a person's birth. Then go to the right end, make an X out of the black tape, and stick it there. Explain that the X represents a person's death.

About $^1/_3$ of the way across the line (from the left), make a cross out of the blue tape and put it right above the line. Tell kids that the cross represents the moment when a person becomes a Christian—the moment they are saved.

solo/strike a chord handout

txt it

You may want to give your teens the option of answering these questions both by talking aloud and by texting. As some share their answers, others can text them to you. Read some of their thoughts aloud and build upon their ideas as your group explores these issues together.

hidden track

Encourage teens who may be spiritual seekers to talk with you privately after this session if they would like to know more about what it means to begin a relationship with Jesus.

Invite everyone to tape their index cards to the wall above and below the time line, clustered around the blue cross. Ask teens to explain in simple language what it means to be saved and what happens when a person becomes saved. Correct any misguided information in a gracious manner. You don't want the kids to feel stupid, but at the same time this is the most important information they will ever hear, so it must be accurate.

If teens haven't mentioned it yet, point out that we often think about salvation as being saved from the punishment for our sins—being saved from going to Hell after we die. Invite a volunteer to read aloud Romans 6:23. Have some volunteers add white tape to the line on the wall, starting from the X (representing a person's death) and going to the end of the wall. Have them create an arrow at the end of the line with the white tape. Explain that this line represents the start of eternity for a person. Communicate clearly to kids that when we accept Jesus' forgiveness and commit our lives to him, we have the promise of spending eternity in Heaven with Christ after death. But then explain that salvation doesn't just begin when we die. We focus so much on the awesomeness of going to Heaven we act as if that's when salvation takes effect—but Jesus describes things very differently.

Walk back over to the cross part of your time line and say: According to Jesus, salvation begins the moment we become Christians. Life changes right here. It's not just about what happens when we die—it's about something that's happening right now.

Start a piece of white tape on top of the time line beginning at the cross. Stretch it across the time line all the way to the X until it connects with the eternity line kids have already created. As you do, tell kids that eternal life itself doesn't begin at death—it begins at the moment a person accepts Jesus as Lord and Savior. Salvation is not something we wait for and receive when we die. It is something very real in this life.

Say: Salvation is God working in us right now, drawing us closer to him, forgiving us, helping us grow and mature in our faith. It's God recreating us, day by day, making something fresh and new out of our lives. The Christian life is not just about a promise of Heaven in the future. Rather, the Christian life is one of completeness, fulfillment, and joy despite hardships we might face in this life. When we have Jesus in our lives, everything is different. 🦋

encore · about 10 minutes

Divide teens into pairs and give each team a "Word Pictures" handout, several multi-colored index cards, and pens. Prompt them to follow the instructions on the handout, discuss the questions, and write down their thoughts on the index cards.

Word Pictures handout

After about 5 minutes, invite everyone to gather around the time line and tape their cards all along the white line stretching between the cross and the X. Then read some of the cards aloud. Teach from what you see written there, drawing out and emphasizing the most important ideas and affirming your jr. highers for what they've written. Invite group members to respond and discuss some follow-up questions based on what you read on the cards.

Emphasize again that God's promises are not only about the future, but are also part of our present reality. 🦋

playlist

To add a relaxing atmosphere in the background during **backstage pass**, download these songs to your iPod (or to a CD) and play them while teens talk:
"Light (Remix)"
by Shawn McDonald
"Captivated (Remix)"
by Shawn McDonald

backstage pass `about 8 minutes`

Summarize again the 2 main ideas of this study. First, God is creating even today. He is at work and calling us to spiritual life. Second, salvation is a present reality. We can find fulfillment in Christ, here and now. It is not just a future promise.

Bring out the pitcher of water, cups, loaf of bread, candle, and matches. Light the candle, and say: These are all important items for people living at any time in history. Water, bread, and light are necessities for life. Jesus takes these powerful symbols to another level. He doesn't just say, "I am water" or "I am bread." He says he's the living water, the bread of life, and the light of life. In other words, Jesus doesn't just sustain us and nourish us and provide for our physical needs, but he does these things for us spiritually. He is essential—he is what we need—for our spiritual lives.

Invite kids to move into a time of worship-focused sharing as they think about the ways God is at work in their own lives. Pass around the bread, cups, and water, inviting teens to eat and drink.

Ask kids to share examples of things God has done in their lives. This should be a loose and open conversation, allowing kids to share whatever God brings to mind for them. If there are moments of quietness, that's fine. To help guide the conversation or get things started, you may want to ask questions like:

✱ How have you felt God at work in your life, recreating you or doing something new in you?

✱ How has Jesus provided for you or nourished you? Share a recent example.

* How has Jesus been refreshing for you?
* How has Jesus brought satisfaction, meaning, or purpose to your life?
* When you think about your relationship with Jesus, what do you want to thank him for?
* Do you feel like you've been living the new life Jesus calls you to? How do you want to change? *

hit the road `about 5 minutes`

Say: Scripture speaks of the believer in Christ as a new creation (2 Corinthians 5:17). We are told that we need to be born again (John 3:3) and to put on the new self (Ephesians 4:24). This is a process. This isn't something that we get right or that makes perfect sense to us the moment we become Christians. If we're believers in Jesus, we're all in the process of changing and maturing. God is at work re-creating us, guiding us, growing us.

Emphasize again to your jr. highers that they have great worth and purpose because they were created by God. Reaffirm that they are made in God's image. Highlight again that they are a new creation—spiritually made new when they place their faith in Jesus.

Wrap up with a time of prayer. If your teens feel comfortable, keep it open for participants to pray aloud. If they're likely to stay silent, lead the prayer yourself, asking God to help kids discover the new life God has called them to.

Let your kids know you'll be sending **5 for 5 world tour** life application and devotional challenges for them to do each day via

5 for 5 world tour handout

aftr u meet

Right after your meeting, send kids the first **5 for 5 world tour** challenge for them to do tomorrow via Twitter, e-mail, or by posting it on a Facebook page (or youth group Web page) you've set up. Continue to send 1 challenge each day for the 5 days following your meeting.

About 2 days after your group meets, send a text message to your kids, encouraging them to live the new life God has called them to. Prompt them to keep at it with their **5 for 5 world tour** challenges and let them know you're praying for them.

Twitter, e-mail, or through a Facebook group you've set up. (Or, if you prefer not to use these technology options, pass out copies of the **5 for 5 world tour** handout you've downloaded from the CD-ROM to the teens.) Encourage your kids to strive to spend about 5 minutes each day connecting with God through these devotional experiences.

My New Job

The Prep

Session goal: Jr. highers will consider the high cost of discipleship and the intense level of commitment Jesus challenged his followers to have.

Scriptures: Matthew 16:24, 25; Matthew 28:19; Luke 14:25-35; Philippians 3:7-11

You'll need:

* Bibles
* Pens or pencils
* Scissors
* Envelopes (1 per every 2 kids)
* 1 piece of poster board
* Markers
* Sticky notes (1 per kid)
* Water-soluble markers

Download and print:

* **solo/strike a chord** discussion guide (1 per kid)
* "Trades of the Old World" handout (1 per every 2 kids)

Optional supplies:

✦ For **backstage pass:** CD player and CD or iPod with the recommended **playlist** song.
✦ For **hit the road**: Download and print copies of this week's **5 for 5 world tour** take-home page (1 per teen) if you are unable to use the technology options.

Setting it up:

✦ Cut apart the words and phrases on the "Trades of the Old World" handouts. Place each set in an envelope.
✦ In large print, write the word "Disciple" on the piece of poster board.
✦ If you'd like to use the optional **playlist** recommendation, download "Revolution" by Worth Dying For and ready your iPod or burn a CD in order to play the song during the session.

Leader insight:

If you've been in youth ministry for more than a year, you've seen the dangerous "high-low" cycle that naturally follows great events like weekend retreats, conferences, concerts, etc. Kids have such an amazing time that quickly upon their return home their "real life" begins to feel like a big disappointment.

Excitement after big events is a great thing, but it can also lead to some dangerous misunderstandings that hurt one's faith rather than help it. In Luke 14, there are lots of people really excited about Jesus. They've heard about his miracles (or seen them). They've listened to his amazing stories. They are pumped up! Luke 14:25 tells us, "A large crowd was following Jesus." This shows us that there was at least some level of commitment there. These people are making the effort to go from place to place to hear more from Jesus and see more miraculous things.

But instead of working up the crowd with another show-stopping miracle, Jesus purposefully cuts through the hype and excitement. With 3 powerful teachings, Jesus gets across a convicting point: Following him is *not* about excitement or hype. In fact, it's a measured, sober commitment. It's something that's done with a level of understanding of the *cost* of discipleship. According to Jesus, only a fool would try to start a building project without gathering the necessary supplies and understanding what it would take to build it—such fools won't succeed! Often we see the spiritual parallel of this among teens who make "commitments" to Jesus on impulse during an exciting event, but who aren't able to follow through because they haven't understood what it really costs to follow Christ.

In this study, you'll help kids focus on what Jesus said about the intensity and focus involved in committing to follow him. They'll dive in by looking at 1 of Jesus' most dicey teachings: "If you want to be my disciple, you must hate everyone else by comparison— your father and mother...brothers and sisters—yes, even your own life. Otherwise, you cannot be my disciple" (Luke 14:26). It's easy to misunderstand Jesus here, but we know from the context of Christ's other teachings that this isn't meant literally; instead, Jesus is purposefully using hyperbole to make the point that is at the heart of this study. Essentially, he is saying that we must love everyone else—even ourselves—less than we love him.

What about you? Do you love all others less than Christ? Are you as committed to him as he calls you to be? Have you made following Christ your primary vocation (calling) in life? How are you modeling a disciple's life to the kids in your small group?

In preparation for leading this small group session, pray: God, I look forward to what you are going to do as we explore discipleship together through this study. Use me, God, to model what it means to be a follower of you. Help me model the life of a disciple to my young "apprentices." Allow me to sense your leading as we explore your Word through this study. In Jesus' name, amen.

b4 u meet

A couple of days before your group meets, send a text message to your kids reminding them of the upcoming Speak study. (If some teens don't text, send them an e-mail or a message on Facebook or MySpace.)

The Session

Rearrange or delete sections of the study to best meet your group's needs.

txt a frnd   about 5 minutes

Invite your small group to consider this question:

❊ If you could have any job in the world, what would it be, and why?

When they've got an answer, invite them to get out their cell phones and text their answer to another person in the room. (If kids don't have their own phone, they could borrow a friend's or could form pairs and talk about their answer to this question.)

When you're ready to move on to the next part of the study, have them put their cell phones away for now. ❊

mic check   about 10 minutes

Trades of the Old World handout

Ask kids to pair up, and give each pair an envelope containing the words and phrases from the "Trades of the Old World" handout. Invite kids to try to match each job description to the proper trade title. When pairs are ready, reveal how many of their answers are correct (for example, "You've got 7 right out of 12"). *Don't* tell them which specific answers are right or wrong. Allow for several rounds of moving the definitions about. If they aren't all able to do so by the time there's just 1 minute left, wrap things up by revealing the correct answers.

Old World Trades Answer Key

Chandler: One who makes candles
Cobbler: A shoemaker, mender
Cooper: One who makes or repairs barrels
Embosser: One who decorates items through engraving or molding
Limner: A portrait painter
Luthier: A person who makes and repairs stringed instruments
Mercer: One who sells fabric
Smelter: A metal worker
Tailor: A maker of clothes
Tanner: One who makes leather out of animal hides
Wainwright: One who builds and repairs wagons
Weaver: A person who makes baskets

Say: In the old world, people did not go off to college to learn how to become an engineer or a carpenter; back then, a trade was learned by simply working alongside your instructor—as an apprentice. Most professions were learned though family relationships. If your father was a carpenter, you would most likely learn from him how to be a carpenter. As you watched and learned as a child, you would learn more skills and take on more responsibilities. Eventually, you would begin working on your own and someday you'd train your own apprentice. We typically don't learn jobs that way today, but there is a way that we can use this apprentice idea in our lives.

solo/strike a chord handout

solo   about 5 minutes

Tell your kids you'd like them to find a spot in your meeting area where they can be alone and spend about 5 minutes reading Scripture and thinking about what it means.

Remind them that last week they learned about living the new life that God has called them to. Now they'll read more about what that means.

Give each teen a copy of the **solo/strike a chord** handout and a pen or pencil, inviting them to read and follow the instructions.
(Have them read through only the top portion, **solo**, right now and they'll need the **strike a chord** portion in a few minutes.) Here's a copy of what they'll read:

Take 5 minutes to read Matthew 28:19 and Luke 14:25-35. Consider:
✷ What do you think it means to "make disciples"?
✷ From the Luke passage, what are some essential truths that Jesus' followers learned about what it means to be a disciple? (Some of the things Jesus says in this passage can be confusing or hard to fully understand, but do your best to put what you think Jesus means into your own words.)

When the kids understand what they're supposed to do, have them take off and find a spot to read and reflect. After about 5 minutes, call everybody back together. ✤

freestyle `about 8 minutes`

txt it

You may want to give your teens the option of texting their answers to the questions to you during your discussion time. Read out loud some of their answers and use them as springboards for further discussion.

Separate kids into groups of 3, and give each group 3 sticky notes. Explain that together they will decide what they think the 3 important characteristics of a disciple are, based on the Luke 14:25-35 passage. Then they should write 1 characteristic on each sticky note. While they are working, post the "Disciple" poster board on a wall with blank space around it.

When kids are finished working, invite them to stick their definitions on the "Disciple" poster. Read aloud the definitions they posted. It's okay if some of the answers are the same—it just reinforces the point. When you're finished reading the definitions, ask the group:

❋ Which definition really stands out to you and helps you understand what it means to be a disciple? Why? ❋

strike a chord `about 15 minutes`

Acknowledge to kids that you realize Jesus says some stuff in Luke 14:25, 26 that is tough to understand at first glance. Explain that they're going to discuss the passage as a group by creating and then answering their own discussion questions about it.

Have the group now look at the bottom portion of the **solo/strike a chord** handout and use it to guide your small group Bible exploration and discussion together as a group.

solo/strike a chord handout

txt it

If you want, invite kids to answer these questions both by talking aloud and by texting. As some share their answers, others can text them to you. Read some of their thoughts aloud and build upon their ideas as your group explores this topic together.

Here's a copy of the **strike a chord** text for you to use to guide your discussion time:

Reread Luke 14:25-35 together. Take a minute or 2 for everyone to write down a discussion question about the passage. Zero in on a few verses that are hard to understand or explore key ideas. An example might be:

✱ Does Jesus really want us to give up everything? What does he mean by that?

Allow time for some teen-led discussion, using their questions. Some may be great questions, and some may be duds. But affirm them for trying, and draw out the best discussion you can from the group in response to the various questions. As your jr. highers "lead," they'll learn at an even deeper level.

After some good discussion time, you may want to ask some follow-up questions if kids haven't zeroed in on the main ideas of the passage. For example, you may want to ask questions like:

✱ Does Jesus really want us to hate our families? What does he really mean in verse 26?

✱ Jesus said in verse 26 that we must hate even our own lives in order to be his disciple. What does he mean by that?

✱ What does it mean to "count the cost" in verse 28? ✱

encore   about 6 minutes

Tell kids that the old world trades, just like the jobs we have today, were ways of making a living. It's not the old world trades themselves so much that we're interested in today, but the apprenticeships they offered, where people learned by living and working alongside someone else—like Jesus' disciples did.

Read Matthew 16:24, 25 aloud. Explain that Jesus' disciples weren't making a living; they were Jesus' apprentices and were actually doing something that might end their lives. All but 2 of the disciples ended up dying as martyrs.

Refer to the characteristics of a disciple that kids posted on the wall. Point out that being a disciple—a true Jesus-follower—isn't about liking Christian music or going to youth group or to camp or to a fun retreat. It isn't about acting a certain way or avoiding certain behaviors.

Challenge kids to be a true disciple: someone who is willing to give her very life for her faith, someone who finds his primary worth, value, joy, and purpose in Jesus, someone who is willing to put her relationship with God way ahead of other relationships with family or friends. A true disciple is someone who sees his faith not just as a part of his life, but as the central "job" of his life.

Then ask the following questions:

✴ How can you live out your role as a disciple of Jesus while you're at school, at home, or at your job?

✴ When you think about what we've discussed about what it means to follow Jesus, how do you sense God might be calling you or challenging you to follow him? ✴

backstage pass about 8 minutes

Invite everyone to pair up and give each pair some water-soluble markers. Challenge teens to share with their partner a specific com-

playlist

To add some powerful ambiance to this prayer experience, download the following song to your iPod (or to a CD) and play it while teens work and pray. Encourage them to listen to the words as well. "Revolution" by Worth Dying For

mitment they want to make to live as a disciple based on today's study. Prompt them to be honest, open, and specific.

Then have partners use the markers to draw a cross on each other's forearm, hand, or ankle. They can take their time making it cool or can be light-hearted about it, but the point here is for kids to support each other in their commitment to focus their lives on the cross.

Then have kids pray with and for their partners, asking God to help them be committed to being a disciple and making disciples, and praying specifically about the life application commitments they've made. ✳

aftr u meet

Right after your meeting, send kids the first **5 for 5 world tour** challenge for them to do tomorrow via Twitter, e-mail, or by posting it on a Facebook page (or youth group Web page) you've set up. Continue to send 1 challenge each day for the 5 days following your meeting.

About 2 days after your group meets, send a text message to your kids, encouraging them to be true disciples as they go throughout their daily lives. Prompt them to keep at it with their **5 for 5 world tour** challenges and let them know you're praying for them.

hit the road   `about 3 minutes`

Read Philippians 3:7-11 from your Bible. Then say something like: As you've been learning, God formed you and set you apart. He's given you a message to speak to the world! You can speak that message not only with the words you say, but also with the way you live. The most powerful message you can send to others is letting them see clearly that Jesus is the central focus of your life. You "make disciples" by telling your friends about God and his work in your life, but also by modeling for others what it means to follow Jesus. As your friends see you following Christ, they can come alongside you and learn from you. They can come to follow Jesus, too.

Let your kids know you'll be sending **5 for 5 world tour** life application and devotional challenges for them to do each day via Twitter, e-mail, or through a Facebook group you've set up. (Or, if you prefer not to use these technology options, pass out copies of the **5 for 5 world tour** handout you've downloaded from the CD-ROM to the teens.) Encourage your kids to strive to spend about 5 minutes each day connecting with God through these devotional experiences. ✦

5 for 5 world tour handout

Picked for God's Team

The Prep

Session goal: Jr. highers will discover that answering God's call isn't about one's personal skills or abilities, but about one's faithfulness and obedience.

Scriptures: Jeremiah 1:4-19; Amos 7:10-17; Mark 6:3; Luke 1:26-38; Luke 1:46-55; Luke 16:10; John 8:41

You'll need:

* Bibles
* Pens or pencils
* Paper
* Tape
* An "intellectual" game (such as Trivial Pursuit)
* Supplies for a "physical skill" game (like darts or ping-pong)

Download and print:

* "Amos" handout (1 copy)
* "Mary" handout (1 copy per kid)
* **solo/strike a chord** discussion guide (1 copy per kid)

Optional supplies:

* For **encore:** TV, DVD player or VCR, and *The Lord of the Rings: The Fellowship of the Ring* movie.
* For **backstage pass:** CD player and CD or iPod with the recommended **playlist** song.

✦ For **hit the road:** Download and print copies of this week's **5 for 5 world tour** take-home page (1 per teen) if you are unable to use the technology options.

Setting it up: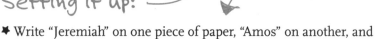

✦ Write "Jeremiah" on one piece of paper, "Amos" on another, and "Mary" on another.
✦ If you'll be showing the movie clip from *The Lord of the Rings: The Fellowship of the Ring,* cue the movie to 1:29:20 (based on 0:00:00 at studio logo).
✦ If you'd like to use the optional **playlist** recommendation, download the song "I Know You're Calling" by Jeremy Camp and ready your iPod or burn a CD in order to play the song during the session.

Leader insight:

It's the moment kids learn to dread in elementary school: the horrific exercise called "picking teams." Usually some really athletic or super brainy kid gets to be the captain and select team members for a sport or academic competition. And the kids who aren't quite coordinated enough or smart enough get picked dead last. You'll *partly* replicate this experience in this study, but without anyone being picked last. The discomfort some kids might feel at the start of the team-picking exercise will serve a purpose later in the session.

See, God *doesn't* pick his "team" that way. He doesn't evaluate to see who's most impressive, smartest, best, or most likely to win. In fact, if you look at the track record in Scripture, God often seems to call the *least* likely candidates. The people God uses are often commonplace, average nobodies who stand out in 1 major way: faithfulness.

You'll use this study to build upon last week's exploration of following God with a deep-rooted commitment. Here kids will consider God's call upon their life: the call to live in faithful obedience in the here and now, and also the "bigger" call he might have on them to do something courageous, new, or different. Teens will look at the examples of Jeremiah, Amos, and Mary as they think about their own personal response to God's call.

So what about you? Are you willing to let your reputation be damaged or gossiped about because of your commitment to Christ (like Mary)? Are you willing to be considered unsuccessful and obey God even without tangible results (like Amos)? Do you find confidence and security in God's power and plan rather than in your own abilities (like Jeremiah)?

As you plan to lead this study, prayerfully consider how God may be calling you to demonstrate faithfulness in the little things—and surrender your heart to him as you seek to be faithful in the big things too. Pray: God, you've called me to minister to these teens. It's a tremendous responsibility. God, I'm humbled that you've chosen me. Help me to always rely on you as the source of my ministry. Guide my words and direct my steps. Strip away any pride I take in my own abilities, and help me keep my focus on you as the center of it all. Speak to me and through me as I lead these teens. In Jesus' name, amen. ✦

b4 u meet

A couple of days before your group meets, send a text message to your kids reminding them of the upcoming Speak study. (If some teens don't text, send them an e-mail or a message on Facebook or MySpace.)

The Session

Rearrange or delete sections of the study to best meet your group's needs.

txt a frnd `about 5 minutes`

Invite your small group to consider this question:

✦ If you could serve God in any way possible—
with money, location, education, your age,
etc., not being an issue—what would you do?

When they've got an answer, invite them to get out their cell phones and text their answer to another person in the room. (If kids don't have their own phone, they could borrow a friend's or could form pairs and talk about their answer to this question.)

When you're ready to move on to the next part of the study, have them put their cell phones away for now. ✦

mic check `about 7 minutes`

Bring out the "intellectual" game and set it in front of the group, but don't say anything. Next, bring out the supplies for the "physical skill" game and set them in front of the group, but still don't say anything.

Select 2 random kids to come up front and tell them that they are going to pick teams for the competition. Without giving *any clues* about what the competition will be, have the team captains begin picking team members, 1 at a time. (Don't worry—this "picking teams" aspect of the activity is part of the point they'll explore later in the session.) Allow them to continue until they've collectively picked about $^2/_3$ of the kids and there is $^1/_3$ of the group left. Interrupt the picking of teams at this point and say that the remaining group (about $^1/_3$ of your kids) will be the 3rd team in the competition.

Once the 3 teams are set, explain that they won't be playing either of the games you set out. Instead they're having a Rock-Paper-Scissors tournament.

Lead the kids in a single-elimination tournament. They simply need to pair up with someone who is *not* on their team and play a round of the game. Whoever loses is "out" and must sit down. (If partners tie, they should play again until there is a winner.) Winners then pair up with another standing player who is not on their team. Continue until there is a single winner. (At some point kids will need to play against their own team members.)

Once you have a winner, exuberantly congratulate him or her as champion and declare that person's team as the winning team. The key idea here is that this competition (unlike the "intellectual" game or the "physical skill" game) had *nothing* to do with skill. This should be obvious to your jr. highers, but don't point it out overtly yet. Instead, continue to ham it up by humorously interviewing the winner before the group as if they possessed an amazing skill that propelled them to the top of the game. Ask the champion questions such as:

✱ So what was it that made you a champion today?

✱ How did you prepare?

✱ Was there any secret to your method?

Lead the group in applauding the winner, then have him or her take a seat. ✤

solo/strike a chord handout

solo   about 5 minutes

Tell your kids you'd like them to find a spot in your meeting area where they can be alone and spend about 5 minutes reading Scripture and thinking about what it means.

Remind them that last week they learned about what it means to be God's disciple. This week they'll be learning about how God chooses people for the tasks he has for them. They will look at the lives of several people in the Bible as examples.

Give each teen a copy of the **solo/strike a chord** handout and a pen or pencil, inviting them to read and follow the instructions. (Have them read through only the top portion, **solo**, right now and they'll need the **strike a chord** portion in a few minutes.) Here's a copy of what they'll read:

Take 5 minutes to read Jeremiah 1:4-19 and Amos 7:10-17. Consider:

🍀 What did God call each of these men to do?

🍀 What stands out to you most from each passage? Why?

When the kids understand what they're supposed to do, have them take off and find a spot to read and reflect. After about 5 minutes, call everybody back together. 🍀

strike a chord ▮about 15 minutes▮

solo/strike a chord handout

Ask a volunteer to reread Jeremiah 1:4-19 aloud.

Say: The example of Jeremiah's calling is a reminder of God's authorship in our lives. He is the author not only of the details of our lives, but also of our calling. God reminds Jeremiah in verse 5, "Before you were born I set you apart." God set Jeremiah apart—he chose Jeremiah. Though the scale of Jeremiah's ministry is far beyond most people's, this Scriptural truth also applies to each of us. The all-knowing, all-powerful, ever-present God chooses and calls us.

Explain the following points in your own words:

✤ When we know that it is God who calls us, it should give us amazing confidence as we take on our mission! We can pursue God's purpose for our lives with resilience, perseverance, and courage.

✤ God says to Jeremiah in verse 9, "I have put my words in your mouth." It's so easy for us to lose sight of this. But God is not only the author of our calling and purpose, he is also the author of our *efforts*. If we are going to be effective, then we must allow God to work in and through us. We need to be more focused on our relationship with him than with outward signs of success or productivity.

✤ We ought to carry out our mission while keeping our eyes on the author of our mission, not on the mission "field."

Have the group now look at the first part of the bottom portion of the **solo/strike a chord** handout and use it to guide your small group Bible exploration and discussion together as a group. Here's a copy of the **strike a chord** text for you to use to guide your discussion time:

txt it

If you want, invite kids to answer these questions both by talking aloud and by texting. As some share their answers, others can text them to you. Read some of their thoughts aloud and build upon their ideas as your group explores this topic together.

Amos handout

| Amos |
| Hi, I'm Amos. God gave me the task of speaking against the people of Israel and their way of life. See, the rich Israelites were abusing their position of wealth. They were oppressing the poor and all the while were carrying on their religious rituals without heartfelt devotion. Needless to say, God had had enough! So he sent me to warn them and demand their repentance.
The weird thing about this, though, is that I'm not a professionally trained prophet. I'm a shepherd. Yep, a shepherd...and a gardener. Not really someone you'd think would be picked to be a prophet, huh? You would think God would choose a well-known speaker or politician, but no, he picked me.
But here's the thing—I'm not really a successful prophet, either. I do what God says, but nobody listens. They ignore me and tell me to go away. But you know what? God has a different view of success than the world does. The results aren't what's important—it's our faithfulness and obedience to answer God's call, no matter how large or small the task. That's what really matters.
speak · Session 5 |

Discuss Jeremiah 1:4-19 together:

✤ In what ways has God been nudging you toward something, such as a ministry he wants you to get involved in, a leadership position he wants you to take on, or a friend he wants you to talk to about Jesus?

✤ What makes it difficult for you to take on that calling and pursue it fully?

✤ How does focusing on God as the author of your mission help you understand the idea of what it means to be "called" by God?

Reread Amos 7:10-17 while kids follow along in their Bibles. Then give the "Amos" handout to 1 teen to read aloud.

Have the group now look at the final part of the bottom portion of the **solo/strike a chord** handout and use it to guide your discussion. Here's a copy of the text to help guide this discussion time:

Discuss Amos 7:10-17 together:

✤ Have you ever felt God leading you to do something that ended up feeling "unsuccessful," like Amos was called to do? Explain.

✤ Did you feel at peace because you obeyed God even though things didn't turn out how you wanted? Why or why not?

✤ What's your reaction to the idea that faithfulness—not success—is the most important thing about responding to God's call in your life? ✤

encore   `about 5 minutes`

Explain that you're going to show a movie clip that emphasizes some of the themes you've been talking about. Say: In this scene, a really important task needs to be done. Very quickly, people start jostling for the job. They each have their own ideas about who is best qualified to take on this mission.

Show the clip from *The Lord of the Rings: The Fellowship of the Ring* beginning at about 1:29:20 (based on 0:00:00 at studio logo) when Elrond says, "The ring cannot be destroyed..." Stop the clip at about 1:33:25 when Pippin says, "Great. Where are we going?"

Say: In many ways, Frodo was the least qualified for the mission. He had no training or battle experience. He didn't have political power or a grand reputation. He was small, quiet, and confused. But he was the one who was chosen for the mission. In Frodo's case, being the least qualified is what made him the most qualified.

God calls people who are dependent on him. It's not about being popular, skilled or the best at something. It's about being faithful in your relationship with Christ. 🍂

backstage pass   `about 10 minutes`

Read Luke 1:26-38 aloud while kids follow along in their own Bibles. Give each kid a copy of the "Mary" handout to read and think about silently.

Mary handout

playlist

To add some ambiance to this experience, download "I Know You're Calling" by Jeremy Camp to your iPod (or to a CD) and play it while teens reflect on the "Mary" handout.

After kids have had a few minutes to read and think about the passage, invite them to close their eyes as you read Mary's song from Luke 1:46-55. Encourage them to make it a personal prayer of praise to God. ✦

txt it

You may want to give your teens the option of texting their reasons for choosing the person they did. Read some of their answers out loud and use them as springboards for further discussion.

freestyle about 8 minutes

Tape the "Jeremiah" sign on one wall, the "Amos" sign on another, and the "Mary" sign on another. Tell kids to choose which of these 3 people they relate to the most and sit under that person's sign. Give them 2 minutes to talk to each other within their groups about why they chose that person. Then ask 1 person from each group to summarize why the people in their group chose the person they did.

Then give kids paper and pencils and instruct them to write down their answers to the following questions:

✦ How do you feel God may be calling you right now (or in the future)?
✦ In light of what you've learned, how do you want to respond to God's call? ✦

hit the road about 5 minutes

Invite a volunteer to read aloud Luke 16:10, and then say: I believe that what we find in today's examples from Scripture are people going about their business faithfully until God interrupted their world. They were faithful with little—faithful in their everyday lives. So God called them to do something really big.

This isn't about some phenomenal calling, like God telling you to become a missionary in Siberia—though he may do that. The main idea here is that we ought to be faithfully carrying out the mission right in front of us: serving God obediently in our everyday lives and waiting expectantly to hear and follow God's directions, no matter how huge or how small that mission might seem. We are to be faithful with the little things, such as praying, seeking God, obeying our parents, showing kindness, and so on. God is honored by our faithfulness—and it prepares us for the greater callings he may have in store for us.

Remember, when we read about people in the Bible, we often only see the exciting times in these people's lives. What we don't see is their day-to-day faithfulness of living holy and pleasing lives before God. These stories are only snapshots of a bigger picture of obedience.

God is calling you. He's chosen you. It's not because you're great at soccer, singing, or math. God calls you not because of your abilities, but because of his ability to work through you.

Follow his call. Obey his instructions. Live a faithful life.

Let your kids know you'll be sending **5 for 5 world tour** life application and devotional challenges for them to do each day via Twitter, e-mail, or through a Facebook group you've set up. (Or, if you prefer not to use these technology options, pass out copies of the **5 for 5 world tour** handout you've downloaded from the CD-ROM to the teens.) Encourage your kids to strive to spend about 5 minutes each day connecting with God through these devotional experiences. 🌿

aftr u meet

Right after your meeting, send kids the first **5 for 5 world tour** challenge for them to do tomorrow via Twitter, e-mail, or by posting it on a Facebook page (or youth group Web page) you've set up. Continue to send 1 challenge each day for the 5 days following your meeting.

About 2 days after your group meets, send a text message to your kids, encouraging them to be faithful and obedient to God in all things. Prompt them to keep at it with their **5 for 5 world tour** challenges and let them know you're praying for them.

5 for 5 world tour handout

6

What Are My Spiritual Gifts?

‗ The Prep ‗

Session goal: Jr. highers will learn about spiritual gifts and will consider the ways God wants to use his power to work through them in the church and in the world.

Scriptures: 1 Corinthians 12, 13; 1 Timothy 1:18-20; 1 Timothy 6:10-21; 2 Timothy 1:1-14

You'll need:

* Bibles
* Pens or pencils
* Paper
* Index cards
* Envelopes (1 per teen)
* Stamps (1 per teen)

Download and print:

* "Spiritual Gifts" handout (1 per kid)
* "Timothy's Story" handout (1 copy; cut apart)
* **solo/strike a chord** discussion guide (1 per kid)

Optional supplies:

* For **backstage pass:** CD player and CD or iPod with the recommended **playlist** song.
* For **hit the road:** Download and print copies of this week's **5 for 5 world tour** take-home page (1 per teen) if you are unable to use the technology options.

Setting it up:

✦ If you'd like to use the optional **playlist** recommendation, download "Use Me" by Dave Hunt and ready your iPod or burn a CD in order to play the song during the session.

Leader insight: ⁻

You're about to embark on an exploration of one of the more controversial matters of Scripture: spiritual gifts. This study avoids discussion of the various perspectives taken on "sign gifts" (tongues, prophecy, etc.). We recommend that if kids are interested you study this topic further at a later date to help them explore your church's understanding of these issues.

But there's another "controversy" about spiritual gifts that you *will* need to think about and discuss during this study: it's the basic definition of what a spiritual gift is. There are 2 main understandings of spiritual gifts. One we'll label as the "What are your strengths?" understanding. This is probably the more common view of gifts in the church today, and it's attested to by countless spiritual gifts inventories and tests you can purchase from various ministries. In this approach people figure out their spiritual gift(s) by looking at their strengths or ministry interests. For example, is he a born leader? Then leadership must be his spiritual gift. Or is she a strong evangelist? Then her gift must be evangelism.

The other approach we'll label as the "What are your weaknesses?" understanding. In this perspective, spiritual gifts are made evident when we are enabled to do something with God's help in an area of our natural weaknesses. For example, Moses was a very poor speaker and felt completely inadequate to confront Pharaoh, but God gifted him to be the leader he never thought he could be. In this view we discover our spiritual gifts when we obey God's leading and trust in his power to help us accomplish his will. We step into situations in which we know beyond a shadow of a doubt that it is God and not our own abilities at work. For example, someone may timidly share his faith, nervously faltering all the while, yet his friend accepts Christ! In that case, he knew the Holy Spirit was at work—he was supernaturally gifted as an evangelist.

So which approach is right and which is wrong? Well, we think *both* are true. A scriptural case can be made for both understandings, and you'll find them each alluded to in this study. When both views are understood in tandem, a more well-rounded understanding of spiritual gifts emerges. God is at work in us through the strengths and passions he's given us *as well as* through our weaknesses and inadequacies.

Timothy takes center stage in this study as an example of a real person who struggled to understand and live out his own spiritual gifts. As you prepare to lead this study, take some time to consider your own spiritual gifts as well as your talents and abilities. Do you struggle with challenges like Timothy did? Fear? Inadequacy? Difficult people? Consider the words of Paul: Fan your gifts into flame. Live boldly with power, love, and self-discipline (2 Timothy 1:6, 7).

In preparation for leading this small group session, pray: Holy Spirit, speak to my jr. highers in a way that I cannot. Show them how you've made them, how you've gifted them, and how you desire to use them. Give them courageous confidence to follow your lead and answer your call. Help me model what it looks like to live a life totally dependent on your power in all things. In Jesus' name, amen. ✺

b4 u meet

A couple of days before your group meets, send a text message to your kids to start thinking about what it means to be gifted for service to God. (If some teens don't text, send them an e-mail or a message on Facebook or MySpace.)

The Session

Rearrange or delete sections of the study to best meet your group's needs.

txt a frnd   about 5 minutes

Distribute index cards and pens to kids. Then, invite your small group to consider this question:

✱ If you could have any superpower imaginable, what would it be?

When they've got an answer, invite them to get out their cell phones and text their answer to another person in the room. (If kids don't have their own phone, they could borrow a friend's or could form pairs and talk about their answer to this question.) The person who receives the text should write the answer down on an index card and hand it to you.

When you're ready to move on to the next part of the study, have them put their cell phones away for now. ✱

mic check   about 7 minutes

Once you've collected all the cards from **txt a frnd**, shuffle them and read through them out loud twice, challenging the group to try to remember all of them. Have everybody stand up in a circle and direct kids to take turns (going around the circle) trying to guess who said what. However, they are not allowed to "guess" the superpower of the person whose answer they wrote down.

If a teen guesses correctly, the person whose answer was guessed should sit down. The guesser then gets another turn.

If a teen guesses incorrectly, the next player gets a turn. Continue around the circle in this way. Kids who are sitting down (because their answer has been guessed) *do* get to take turns guessing as well. The winner of the game is the last person left standing.

When you're finished playing, say: It's unlikely that any of us will ever have any of those superpowers, but God does give us something a bit like superpowers—the Bible calls them spiritual gifts. God gives us abilities to do things through his power—things we couldn't do on our own. ✦

solo about 5 minutes

Tell your kids you'd like them to find a spot in your meeting area where they can be alone and spend about 5 minutes reading Scripture and thinking about what it means.

Remind them that last week they read about 3 people who answered God's calling on their lives. This week they'll discover more about the kinds of things God might call them to do.

Give each teen a copy of the **solo/strike a chord** handout and a pen or pencil, inviting them to read and follow the instructions. (Have them read through only the top portion, **solo**, right now and they'll need the **strike a chord** portion in a few minutes.) Here's a copy of what they'll read:

hidden track

If you only have a few kids, you might want to play another round or 2 of this game, asking questions such as, "If you were a superhero, who would be your sidekick?" or "What would your superhero costume look like?" In order to save time for these rounds, kids should write down their own answers on the cards instead of texting them.

solo/strike a chord handout

Take a few minutes to read 1 Corinthians 12:4-11 and answer this question:

♥ What are the basic things we learn about spiritual gifts from this passage? Write down at least 3 observations.

When the kids understand what they're supposed to do, have them take off and find a spot to read and reflect. After about 5 minutes, call everybody back together. ♥

solo/strike a chord handout

Spirtual Gifts handout

strike a chord   about 10 minutes

Read 1 Corinthians 12:4-11 aloud while kids follow along in their Bibles. Then ask kids what they learned about spiritual gifts from that passage. Make sure to highlight the following points:

1. Every believer receives a spiritual gift.
2. It is given for the edification of the church body and its mission.
3. There is a variety in the types of gifts God gives.
4. The Holy Spirit is the author of these gifts—he determines how, when, and to whom he distributes the gifts.

Give each kid a "Spiritual Gifts" handout, and have the group look at the bottom portion of the **solo/strike a chord** handout and use it to guide your small group Bible exploration and discussion together as a group. Here's a copy of the **strike a chord** text for you to use to guide your discussion time:

Using 1 Corinthians 12:8-10 and your "Spiritual Gifts" handout, answer the following questions:

✱ What are some examples of ways you've seen people use their gifts to build up the church or to fulfill God's mission?

✱ What do you think are the main reasons Christians, both young and old, may fail to use their spiritual gifts or follow their calling?

✱ In your opinion, what do you think is the difference between a talent and a spiritual gift?

txt it

If you want, invite kids to answer these questions both by talking aloud and by texting. As some share their answers, others can text them to you. Read some of their thoughts aloud and build upon their ideas as your group explores this topic together.

Say: God gives us talents and abilities—and he wants to use those in our lives to bring glory to him. These are gifts from God, but often spiritual gifts are different than those natural talents and abilities. A spiritual gift is when God enables us to do something through the power of the Holy Spirit in our lives; it's not necessarily related to our own talents or abilities. It's all about God's ability to work through us.

Ask:

✱ So far in your life, how has God used you to build up the church or to be a part of his mission?

✱ When have you felt like God helped you to do something that you might not have been able to do on your own? ✿

encore about 13 minutes

Tell kids that they'll be learning about a man named Timothy. Explain that the story they will read is fictionalized, but it's based on Scripture. Hand out the pieces of "Timothy's Story" to 9 kids. Ask volunteers to read their sections aloud in order.

Timothy's Story handout

Then read 2 Timothy 1:1-14 aloud while teens follow along in their own Bibles. Instruct kids to look at their "Spiritual Gifts" handout and ask:

🌢 What spiritual gift do you think God gave to Timothy?

Say: Whichever gift—or gifts—God gave to Timothy, we can know that it was the one(s) he needed to lead the church. We know that God does the same for us. He gives us the gifts we need to accomplish the tasks he sets before us.

Outline the truths kids have learned today:

🌢 Every Christian receives at least 1 spiritual gift.

🌢 These gifts are for building up the church and fulfilling God's mission.

🌢 There are a variety of gifts given by the Holy Spirit.

🌢 A person's spiritual gifts are closely connected to living a holy life. 🌢

freestyle about 7 minutes

Ask kids to look at 1 Timothy 1:18-20; 1 Timothy 6:10-21; and 2 Timothy 1:1-14 as they answer the following questions:

🌢 What's your reaction to the story of Timothy's life? What stands out to you most?

🌢 What words, phrases, or ideas struck you from Paul's letters to Timothy?

🌢 If you were Timothy, what effect do you think these letters would have on you? Why? 🌢

txt it

You may want to give your teens the option of texting their answers to these questions to you during your discussion time. Read some of their answers out loud and use them as springboards for further discussion.

backstage pass about 8 minutes

Hand out an envelope, paper, and a pen to each kid and invite everyone to spread out around the room. Instruct kids to write their name and address on the front of the envelope and then invite them to write a letter to themselves. Prompt them to write specifically about how they feel God has been encouraging, challenging, or directing them in their lives through this study series. Encourage them to also write about how they feel God may be gifting them to serve the church and take part in its mission of making disciples.

Warn kids when there is 1 minute left. When time is up, tell kids to put their letters in the envelopes but to *not* seal them yet. Collect the envelopes. Tell the kids that you will be adding something to the envelopes before you mail them out, but that you will not read what they wrote. 🍂

hidden track

Before sealing and mailing the envelopes, write a short note of encouragement to each kid, telling him or her some ways you see their spiritual gifts and how you've seen them use some of their God-given talents and abilities.

playlist

To add some powerful ambiance to this experience, download the following song to your iPod (or burn a CD) and play it while jr. highers write their letters. Encourage them to listen to the words as well. "Use Me" by Dave Hunt

hit the road about 5 minutes

Say: God has given you a spiritual gift. You may already know what it is, or you may discover it when you live out your calling and you notice God's power helping you along the way. Remember, as we follow Jesus and answer his call, he doesn't leave us on our own to falter and fail! He gives us the power of his Spirit to accomplish his purposes for us. As you seek to live a holy life and are committed to following Jesus, God

aftr u meet

Right after your meeting, send kids the first **5 for 5 world tour** challenge for them to do tomorrow via Twitter, e-mail, or by posting it on a Facebook page (or youth group Web page) you've set up. Continue to send 1 challenge each day for the 5 days following your meeting.

About 2 days after your group meets, send a text message to your kids, encouraging them to consider the ways God wants them to use the gifts he has given them. Prompt them to keep at it with their **5 for 5 world tour** challenges and let them know you're praying for them.

5 for 5 world tour handout

will enable you through spiritual gifts and through his power to do the tasks set before you.

Tell kids to take home their "Spiritual Gifts" handouts. Invite them to think about and pray over the lists as they seek to discover the gift(s) God has given them to use to build up the church and carry out his mission.

Wrap up with a time of prayer. If your jr. highers feel comfortable, keep it open for participants to pray aloud. If they're likely to stay silent, lead the prayer yourself, asking God to inspire and strengthen each of them as they discover and use their spiritual gifts.

Let your kids know you'll be sending **5 for 5 world tour** life application and devotional challenges for them to do each day via Twitter, e-mail, or through a Facebook group you've set up. (Or, if you prefer not to use these technology options, pass out copies of the **5 for 5 world tour** handout you've downloaded from the CD-ROM to the teens.) Encourage your kids to strive to spend about 5 minutes each day connecting with God through these devotional experiences.

7

I'm Supposed to Do WHAT?!

— The Prep —

Session goal:
Jr. highers will examine the biblical imperative to make disciples and will be challenged to both proclaim the gospel with their lives and share the gospel with their words.

Scriptures:
Jeremiah 1:9; Matthew 28:19; Mark 13:11; John 4:27-42; Acts 17:22-34; 2 Timothy 1:7, 8

You'll need:

* Bibles
* Pens or pencils
* Paper

Download and print:

* "Your Power Source" handout (1 per kid)
* **solo/strike a chord** discussion guide (1 per kid)

Optional supplies:

* For **freestyle:** CD player and CD or iPod with recommended **playlist** songs.
* For **hit the road:** Download and print copies of this week's **5 for 5 world tour** take-home page (1 per teen) if you are unable to use the technology options.

Setting it up:

* You will need to prepare a few question sheets for **freestyle.** At the top of a sheet of paper, write 1 of the questions below, allowing enough room for kids to write their answers underneath. Make 2 sheets for each question.
    * what reasons do Christians have for evangelizing?

- What are some of the common fears Christians have about sharing their faith?
- In your opinion, how should a Christian evangelize? What methods or styles are most appropriate?
- What are the most important ideas to share—or questions to ask—when you're talking to someone about your faith in Jesus?

✦ If you'd like to use the optional **playlist** recommendations, download the songs "All the Trees of the Field Will Clap Their Hands," "For the Widows in Paradise, for the Fearless in Ypsilanti," and "The Transfiguration" by Sufjan Stevens, and ready your iPod or burn a CD in order to play the songs during the session.

Leader insight:

As we try to help jr. highers grow spiritually, it's tempting to focus a little *too much* on their personal relationship with Jesus. What? Is that possible?

Sure it is, because focusing too heavily on individual spiritual growth can lead to an off-kilter faith—a perspective that sees Jesus' death on the cross and the blessing of new life as *all about me. Me, me, me.*

But the reality is that true discipleship has a huge component that often gets under-emphasized in modern churches: that following Jesus has more to do with *others* than it has to do with *us.* And a huge component of being others-focused is proclaiming the gospel.

In this study you'll help kids begin to explore what evangelism really means. It's not meant to stand on its own—this session is purposefully meant as a follow-up to the studies you've done about following Jesus with full-hearted commitment and answering his call. After all, the loudest message we proclaim about Christ is the message we deliver with our lives. Teens who are Christlike in their actions and attitudes are living a life-changing message that others will "hear" loud and clear.

But kids will also be challenged with the truth that using words is a necessary part of evangelism. They'll consider 2 different examples of evangelism from Scripture: the simple, pure, and natural evangelism of the Samaritan woman who Jesus spoke to at the well (John 4) and the thorough, strategic explanation of the gospel that Paul proclaimed in Athens (Acts 17). You'll lead your teens to see themselves as evangelists—as those charged with proclaiming the Good News.

What about you? How often do you view yourself as an evangelist? When was the last time you earnestly prayed for a non-Christian friend or family member? How often do you speak naturally with others about your faith in Jesus? Allow your challenge to your kids to also spur you on in your own response to Jesus' call to go and make disciples.

As you prepare to lead your jr. highers through this experience, pray:

Jesus, it sounds so simple to invite my friends to "come and see" who you really are. But in reality it feels so hard. It's even more intimidating for my jr. highers. Empower us through your Holy Spirit to sense your leading in this area and to see the mission you have for each of us in making disciples. May many people be changed by the conversations that will result from this study. In Jesus' name, amen. ✳

The Session

Rearrange or delete sections of the study to best meet your group's needs.

txt a frnd — about 5 minutes

Invite your small group to consider this question:

✤ What is one of your biggest fears?

When they've got an answer, invite them to get out their cell phones and text their answer to another person in the room. (If kids don't have their own phone, they could borrow a friend's or could form pairs and talk about their answer to this question.)

When you're ready to move on to the next part of the study, have them put their cell phones away for now. ✤

mic check — about 8 minutes

Lead everyone in playing the old-fashioned game "Simon Says." To play, give kids simple commands to follow. If you say, "Simon says" at the beginning of a command, they should immediately obey. If you don't say, "Simon says," they should ignore your command.

Play together for 5 or 6 minutes, and make it silly and fun by including goofy instructions like, "Simon says to sing opera," or "Simon Says to hula dance," along with simple instructions like, "Simon says to take 3 steps forward."

Then read Jesus' words in Matthew 28:19 aloud to the group.

Say: This isn't a suggestion from Jesus. This is a command. In the game we just played, the idea was that if "Simon" said it, you did

b4 u meet

A couple of days before your group meets, send a text message to your kids reminding them of the upcoming Speak study. (If some teens don't text, send them an e-mail or a message on Facebook or MySpace.)

it. According to the rules of the game, Simon was king. Without the agreed-upon rules, the game wouldn't work. If no one took what Simon said seriously, the game would be pointless.

Here in Matthew 28:19 we have a command given by Jesus for his people to "make disciples." A few weeks ago we studied what it means to follow Jesus—to be his disciple. Now we want to look even more closely at this idea: What does it really mean to go and make disciples?

Explain that part of what this means is proclaiming the gospel. *Evangelism* is the word we use today for proclaiming the gospel. *Evangel* means "good news." So this big, intimidating word really means something very simple: telling others the good news about Jesus. 🔹

freestyle about 15 minutes

Explain to kids that they're going to get a chance to answer a few questions about evangelism. Read the questions aloud from the sheets you prepared earlier.

Then place the sheets around the room. Insruct kids to write thoughtful, honest answers on the papers for the 2 questions that most grab their interest. Allow about 5 minutes for kids to write their answers.

Collect the sheets and read the answers aloud. Then discuss their answers for each question, using the following:

playlist

To add some powerful ambiance to today's session, download these songs by Sufjan Stevens to your iPod (or to a CD). Sufjan Stevens is an indie-folk-alternative singer who is a committed Christian. Though most of his music does not have overt references to his faith, there are strong Christian overtones to his lyrics. Consider playing the following songs in the background while teens write their answers during **freestyle** and during the other times of writing and reflection in this session.
"All the Trees of the Field Will Clap Their Hands"
"For the Widows in Paradise, for the Fearless in Ypsilanti"
"The Transfiguration"

✱ Which answers do you agree with most? Why?
✱ Do you think any ideas need to be added to the discussion of this question? If so, what?
✱ How does this question relate to your own life? ✱

solo [about 5 minutes]

Tell your kids you'd like them to find a spot in your meeting area where they can be alone and spend about 5 minutes reading Scripture and thinking about what it means.

Remind them that they've been learning about following Jesus with full-hearted commitment and answering his call. Part of that call for every Christian is to make disciples.

Give each teen a copy of the **solo/strike a chord** handout and a pen or pencil, inviting them to read and follow the instructions. (Have them read through only the top portion, **solo**, right now and they'll need the **strike a chord** portion in a few minutes.) Here's a copy of what they'll read:

Take 5 minutes to read John 4:27-42 and Acts 17:22-34. Consider:
✱ What do you think these passages have in common?
✱ What stands out to you most from these passages? Why?

When the kids understand what they're supposed to do, have them take off and find a spot to read and reflect. After about 5 minutes, call everybody back together. ✱

txt it

You may want to give your teens the option of texting their answers to these questions to you during your discussion time. Read some of their answers out loud and use them as springboards for further discussion.

solo/strike a chord handout

solo/strike a chord handout

txt it

If you want, invite kids to answer these questions both by talking aloud and by texting. As some share their answers, others can text them to you. Read some of their thoughts aloud and build upon their ideas as your group explores this topic together.

strike a chord about 10 minutes

Say: The 2 stories you just read are 2 examples of evangelism. Let's take a few minutes to compare and contrast these examples.

Ask kids to pair up. Instruct 1 kid in each pair to look up John 4:27-42, and the other to look up Acts 17:22-34. Having a Bible open to each passage will help them be able to compare the 2 stories.

Have the group now look at the bottom portion of the **solo/strike a chord** handout and use it to guide your small group Bible exploration and discussion together as a group. Here's a copy of the **strike a chord** text for you to use to guide your discussion time:

Look over John 4:27-42 and Acts 17:22-34 together and talk about these questions:

✤ What's similar in these 2 examples?
✤ What's different?
✤ What words, phrases, or descriptions stand out to you?

When kids are finished comparing and contrasting the passages, ask:
✤ How does each example inspire you?
✤ Which example do you identify with most? Why?

encore about 7 minutes

Say: We've talked for several weeks about what it means to be a disciple of Jesus. We're made by God in his image and we're made new by him through faith in Jesus. We commit our lives to follow him and we answer his calling to live out the mission he has for us. He gives us the gifts we need, through his Holy Spirit, to accomplish that mission.

In some ways we'll each have our own unique calling from God, such as the career plans he might have for us or a ministry he wants us to pursue. But we also share a general calling that Jesus has for all of his followers: making disciples.

Re-read Matthew 28:19, then recap the following in your own words:

* An important part of making disciples is following Jesus with our lives. We are called to live a vibrant Christian life in front of others.

* We also learn throughout Jesus' many powerful and convicting teachings that we are to proclaim the gospel through our actions, like service, demonstrating God's love, acts of compassion, embodying justice, and standing up for truth.

* But God calls us to proclaim the gospel *both* with our lives and with our words. Part of proclaiming the gospel *must* involve talking with others about Jesus. There are a variety of ways God might call us to do this. We might mimic the Samaritan woman and keep it simple—just tell people who Jesus is and what he has done for us. Or we can be more strategic, like Paul, who went more in-depth about faith ideas and was aware of the spiritual openness of the people he was talking to.

Say: Think for a moment of some of your non-Christian friends or family members. Where do you see spiritual openness in their lives? For example, do they listen to music that's about how hard, discouraging, and confusing life can be? Then you can point them to the joy and hope that is found in Christ. Do they love the outdoors? Then you can point

hidden track

If you sense that your kids need follow-up training on sharing their faith, you may want to consider checking out James Choung's "Big Story" evangelism tool as explained on his Web site at www.jameschoung.net or in his books *True Story* and *Based on a True Story* (InterVarsity Press). This tool is a new and fresh way of explaining the story of God's plan of salvation in basic terms.

Your Power Source handout

Your Power Source

"For God has not given us a spirit of fear and timidity, but of power, love, and self-discipline. So never be ashamed to tell others about our Lord."

— 2 Timothy 1:7-8

speak · Session 7

---

them to the awesomeness of the creator whose presence we sense when we relax and enjoy nature.

Allow a few minutes for kids to come up with some examples of their own.

Say: It's not always easy to talk about Jesus with friends. Sometimes they might ask questions that trip us up, or they might want to argue with us. When challenges like that come our way, we need to trust in God and listen to his guidance for what to say or simply how to listen. God told Jeremiah "I have put my words in your mouth" (Jeremiah 1:9), and Jesus told the disciples that when they were in tough situations, the Holy Spirit would speak through them and give them the words to say (Mark 13:11). God will guide us as we try to introduce our friends to Jesus. 🍂

backstage pass   about 6 minutes

Direct kids to pair up with another teen in the room they feel comfortable talking with. Prompt them to talk with their partner about 1 or 2 of the evangelism questions they answered earlier that really made them think. As they talk, hand out the "Your Power Source" handout.

Next, ask teens to silently think about specific people God has brought to mind during the study—people who don't have a relationship with Jesus. Allow for about 30 seconds of silence here while the Holy Spirit brings specific people to mind for each jr. higher.

Direct teens to tell their partners about a specific person they feel God might be calling them to share the gospel with. Have kids each read 2 Timothy 1:7, 8 aloud to their partner (it's on the handout) and then pray for each other and the specific relationships they mentioned. ✦

hit the road   `about 4 minutes`

Say: Making disciples is part of our calling. It's not optional. Being a Jesus-follower means that we get to have an awesome, growing relationship with God. It's not all about us and our personal spiritual growth; it's also about others. It's about sharing the gospel through our actions of service and love. It's also about sharing the gospel with our words.

Hold up the question sheets (from **freestyle**) that ask: What are some of the common fears Christians have about sharing their faith?

Say: All of these fears are real. But when they hold us back from sharing the gospel, they stand in the way of us truly following Jesus.

Invite kids to privately think for a moment about how their own fears have held them back from sharing the gospel; allow at least 30 seconds of quietness.

Direct kids to look at their "Your Power Source" handouts, and read the verse aloud together. Then, tear up the question sheets.

As you tear up the question sheets, say: We need to get rid of our fears so they don't hold us back from true discipleship. We should acknowledge our fears and recognize them in our lives, and then ask God to help us have victory over them. We have the power of the Holy Spirit in our lives and no fear can stand up to him. Jesus told us to go and make disciples. We can boldly do so with our lives, with our actions, and with our words.

aftr u meet

Right after your meeting, send kids the first **5 for 5 world tour** challenge for them to do tomorrow via Twitter, e-mail, or by posting it on a Facebook page (or youth group Web page) you've set up. Continue to send 1 challenge each day for the 5 days following your meeting.

About 2 days after your group meets, send a text message to your kids, encouraging them to talk to someone about Jesus that day. Prompt them to keep at it with their **5 for 5 world tour** challenges and let them know you're praying for them.

Wrap up with a time of prayer. If your jr. highers feel comfortable, keep it open for participants to pray aloud. If they're likely to stay silent, lead the prayer yourself, asking God to help each person follow his command to go and make disciples.

Let your kids know you'll be sending **5 for 5 world tour** life application and devotional challenges for them to do each day via Twitter, e-mail, or through a Facebook group you've set up. (Or, if you prefer not to use these technology options, pass out copies of the **5 for 5 world tour** handout you've downloaded from the CD-ROM to the teens.) Encourage your kids to strive to spend about 5 minutes each day connecting with God through these devotional experiences.

5 for 5 world tour handout

Becoming God's Instrument

The Prep

Session goal: Jr. highers will be inspired by Esther being used as an instrument of God's peace and will seek to discover the purposes he has in store for them to be used as his instruments.

Scriptures: Genesis 37; Genesis 39–42; Genesis 44; Genesis 45; Esther 3:8-11; Esther 4:8-16; 1 Corinthians 7:17, 20-24

You'll need:

- ✦ Bibles
- ✦ Pens or pencils
- ✦ Several index cards
- ✦ Pens
- ✦ Roll paper or poster board
- ✦ Marker

Download and print:

- ✦ **solo/strike a chord** discussion guide (1 per teen)
- ✦ "Make Me an Instrument" handout (1 per teen)
- ✦ "Prepared for a Purpose" handout (1 per teen)

Optional supplies:

- ✦ For **mic check:** Various lists of "The Top 10 Inventions of All Time" from the Internet.
- ✦ For **hit the road:** CD player and CD or iPod with the recommended **playlist** song.

✦ For **hit the road:** Download and print copies of this week's **5 for 5 world tour** take-home page (1 per teen) if you are unable to use the technology options.

Setting it up:

✦ You might want to look online to find different people's opinions of what the top 10 inventions of all time have been, to read aloud and compare with your group's ideas during **mic check**.

✦ Prepare a time line of Esther's life on roll paper or poster board. (These events are listed in the **strike a chord** section.)

✦ If you decide to do the optional personal testimony in **encore**, spend some time thinking through how God has used the various circumstances in your life, both positive and negative, to prepare you for jr. high small group ministry and other types of ministry you are doing. Use this as an opportunity to demonstrate specific ways you can see God's leading in your life as you look back upon it in retrospect.

✦ If you'd like to use the optional **playlist** recommendation, download "Instrument of Your Peace" by the Paul Coleman Trio from *City on a Hill: The Gathering* and ready your iPod or burn a CD in order to play the song during the session.

Leader insight:

St. Francis put it very simply when he prayed, "Lord, make me an instrument of thy peace." He expressed an earnest desire to be used by God in his life. It's beautiful, inspiring, and so...so *un-American!*

Our culture often thrives on independence and autonomy. Our lives are *ours* to do with them whatever we see fit. *We* are in the driver's seat. And jr. highers feel this internal drive, especially as they begin the developmental process of *individuation* in which they begin to break away from their parents and establish themselves as individuals.

To pray to become God's instrument is a prayer of complete surrender. It's saying, "God use me as you see fit." It's saying, "Not my will, but yours be done." It's saying, "My life isn't under my control—it's in your hands and meant for your purposes." You couldn't get any more countercultural than that!

In this study, you will examine the life of Esther to discover that God is at work in our lives, shaping and preparing us for his purposes even when we don't realize it. Sure, God works through dramatic moments like conversion or miracles or spiritual highs. But God is also at work through the everyday circumstances in a jr. higher's life, like relating to his parents, getting dumped by his first girlfriend, excelling at math, making friends in his 4th period class, or pitying someone who's a social outcast.

We're often able to see these things in retrospect when we reflect on our past, but how often do we really take the time to think about this? How willing are we to accept our present circumstances—even things we don't like—as part of God's sovereign plan to move us toward spiritual maturation?

During this study, you'll help open kids' eyes to the ministry opportunities God has right before them. You'll help them see that this isn't just about some future career in ministry or some other dramatic excursion from everyday life—this is about God placing them right where he wants them to be to do his work *now*. Like Esther and many others in Scripture, God placed them within their life circumstances in order to *use* them in those circumstances.

How about you? Take some time as you prepare for this study to really think about God's hand at work "behind the scenes" in your life, guiding you, changing you, and maturing you for his purposes.

Consider how he is using you right now and how you may need to make yourself even more available to him and more surrendered to his will and his plans for you.

As you prepare for this study, pray the words of St. Francis and consider how they relate to the people you see each day, the places you go each day, and the uses God may have in mind for you each day. Pray: "Lord, make me an instrument of thy peace. Where there is hatred, let me sow love; where there is injury, pardon; where there is doubt, faith; where there is despair, hope; where there is darkness, light; where there is sadness, joy. O Divine Master, grant that I may not so much seek to be consoled as to console; to be understood as to understand; to be loved as to love. For it is in giving that we receive; it is in pardoning that we are pardoned; and it is in dying that we are born to eternal life." In Jesus' name, amen.

b4 u meet

A couple of days before your group meets, send a text message to your kids reminding them of your next small group time. In your text, invite them to start thinking about ways they have been used by God or how they may wish to be used by God in the future. (If some teens don't text, send them an e-mail or a message on Facebook or MySpace.)

The Session

Rearrange or delete sections of the study to best meet your group's needs.

txt a frnd about 5 minutes

Invite your group to consider this question:
* What's one modern invention you couldn't live without? Why?

When they've got an answer, invite them to get out their cell phones and text their answer to another person in the room. (If kids don't have their own phone, they could borrow a friend's or could form pairs and talk about their answer to this question.)

When you're ready to move on to the next part of the study, have them put their cell phones away for now. *

mic check about 5 to 10 minutes

Have kids work in pairs or trios and give each group an index card and a pen. Say:
Work together to come up with a list of what you think are the top 10 inventions of all time.

Instruct them to rank their list, with 1 being the most important invention. Give them several minutes to work together and complete their lists.

hidden track

You may want to look online for some other people's ideas of the top 10 inventions of all time. You can write down a few or print off some to read with your jr. highers and compare your group's lists with other people's.

When time's up, get everyone's attention. Ask groups to shout out some items from their lists.

Say: **You may have heard the phrase, "Necessity is the mother of invention." This means that a particular object is created in order to solve a problem. All of these inventions were conceived, designed, and produced for specific functions. Their existence was purposeful and intentional.**

Just like an invention is designed for a certain purpose, you are, too. Your abilities, your weaknesses, the good and bad experiences in your life all play a part in the purpose God has in mind for you. Let's explore what it means for each of us to be prepared by God and used by God. 🔸

solo   about 5 minutes

Tell your kids you'd like them to find a spot in your meeting area where they can be alone and spend about 5 minutes reading Scripture and thinking about what it means.

Explain that Esther went through some good and bad experiences in her life, but they all led up to a purpose. Tell them that these Scriptures are where the biggest purpose of her life appeared before her. Give your teens a copy of the **solo/strike a chord** handout and a pen or pencil, inviting them to read and follow the instructions. (Have them read through only the top half, **solo**, right now and they'll need the **strike a chord** portion in a few minutes.) Here's a copy of what they'll read:

Take 5 minutes to read Esther 3:8-11 and Esther 4:8-16 and think about it. Jot down your thoughts, ideas, or questions. Consider:

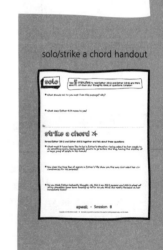

solo/strike a chord handout

✦ What stands out to you most from this passage? Why?

✦ What does Esther 4:14 mean to you?

When your kids understand what they're supposed to do, have them take off and find a spot to read and reflect. After about 5 minutes, call everybody back together. ✦

solo/strike a chord handout

strike a chord   `about 15 minutes`

Say: The Bible is full of example after example of people who God placed right where he wanted them for his purposes. In his plan, all the different circumstances of their lives were part of what he had in store for them. He allowed both good things and very hard things to happen to his people in order to prepare them for the way he wanted to use them. One great example of this is the story of Esther. Let's look at her life for a moment.

Pull out your time line of Esther's life and use it to summarize the events from Esther chapters 1–3:

✦ The setting is Persia, where God's people, the Jews, live as exiles.

✦ Esther is an orphan—both of her parents are dead.

✦ Esther is raised by her cousin Mordecai, who loves her like she is his own daughter.

✦ Esther is very beautiful.

✦ The king wants a new wife and he has all the most beautiful women of the country brought into his harem for him to evaluate.

✦ Esther is taken from her home and put into the harem.

✦ Her cousin Mordecai tells her to keep her identity as a Jew a secret.

* Each woman in the harem got beauty treatments for 12 months, and then she had to spend 1 night with the king. The king would then decide if he liked her or not.
* Esther is chosen by Xerxes to be queen.
* As queen, Esther has a place of honor. At the same time, though, she must be totally subservient to the king. If she were ever to talk to him without his invitation, she could be killed.
* The political situation is very perilous; there is a political leader who is plotting to kill all the Jews in their land.
* Haman convinces the king to have all the Jewish people killed.

Have the group now look at the bottom portion of the **solo/strike a chord** handout and use it to guide your small group Bible exploration and discussion together as a group. Here's a copy of the **strike a chord** text for you to use to guide your discussion time:

Reread Esther 3:8-11 and Esther 4:8-16 together and talk about these questions:

* What must it have been like to be in Esther's situation—being asked by her cousin to do something scary, facing possible death to go before the king, having the destiny of a huge group of people in her hands?

hidden track

You may want to explain here that though the Bible doesn't directly explore this issue, the text and our historical understanding of that time imply that the women had no choice about being taken into the king's harem. After spending a night with the king (and what is assumed here is that they were essentially "forced" into sexual intimacy with him), they became his concubines, which meant they could be used sexually by him without the honor of being his wife. This isn't a fairy tale-like beauty contest. This is something that was likely very difficult for the women on many levels: personally (taken from their families), sexually (Scripture is clear that the women were all virgins; they were likely young as well), and emotionally (knowing that they had only 1 night to "please" the king and that their future place in life depended on it). This would have been especially traumatic for a God-fearing young Jewish girl.

✦ How does the time line of events in Esther's life show you the way God used her circumstances for his purposes?

✦ Do you think Esther instantly thought, *Oh, this is my life's purpose and this is what all of my situations have been leading up to?* Or do you think she mostly focused on her immediate fears?

Explain that Esther had both bad and good in her life. Her parents died and she went through the heartache of being an orphan. She was a part of an ethnic group, the Jews, who were exiles from their homeland and were a persecuted minority in the land where they lived. Also, she was taken from her life and made to live in a harem. On the other hand, she was chosen to be queen. She was suddenly put into a position of power and influence.

Say: Esther was right where God wanted her to be to fulfill his plans at the exact moment he needed. If you read on in the book of Esther, you'll see that God did use Esther to save her people, the Jews, from genocide. ✦

encore about 5 to 10 minutes

If you feel comfortable, briefly share your own testimony about how God has been at work throughout your life, leading, guiding, and preparing you for your current ministry as a jr. high small group leader and for other ministries you may be involved in. Share honestly about both good experiences and bad circumstances or lessons you've learned through sin or other hardships. Emphasize both big events as well as some everyday details. Share how God has formed you in specific areas and guided you to minister to others within the circumstances in which he's placed you.

Then say: When we think about God using us, we often think about people who've been called "away" from their real lives into some amazing ministry. But according to Paul, when a person makes a commitment to follow Christ, that doesn't mean she should try to change her circumstances. Paul teaches that when God calls us to be his instruments, it's often because he wants us to minister within our current circumstances.

Read 1 Corinthians 7:17, 20-24 aloud while everyone follows along in their own Bibles. Then discuss these thoughts:

God *may* call some of us to leave our everyday lives for some exciting ministry like becoming a missionary on the other side of the world. But we need to see our everyday lives as our mission field. We do give up something—we give up our control of our lives and surrender to God, committing to obey him and follow his lead. In this passage we just read, Paul uses a very extreme example—slavery—to stress that even if we live in very difficult circumstances, we should still seek ministry opportunities where we are.

Say: God has prepared you for the ministry he has for you right here, right now. God knows about your family, your friends, your school. God knows your address, your hobbies, and your passions. He wants you to be his instrument in your world. He's not waiting to use you only when you're older. God wants to use you now, right where you are. ✦

freestyle `about 5 minutes`

Ask:
  ✦ What do you do on a typical day?
Prompt kids to share the most basic, mundane stuff—from brushing teeth in the morning to sitting through science class to hanging

txt it

You may want to give your teens the option of texting their answers to you during your discussion time.

out with friends to eating dinner with the family. After a typical day for a jr. higher has been adequately described, ask:

✱ How can you be God's instrument in that world—in that typical day?

Prompt kids to come up with specific ideas. If kids are just quietly thinking, add some examples of your own, such as worshiping God through times of prayer in the morning, honoring God by learning about his world in science class, encouraging a friend at school who is having a bad day, or helping to cook dinner as a way of serving one's family.

Sum up the teaching time by saying: You're called to be faithful in your present situation. You're to make yourself available to God to lead and guide you as you listen to him and follow his will for you. You are God's instrument, and he wants to use you. ✱

Make Me an Instrument handout

backstage pass about 2 to 5 minutes

Pass out the "Make Me an Instrument" handout to each teen and say: The prayer on this handout is based on an ancient prayer written by St. Francis of Assisi, a Christian man who lived in the 1100s.

Invite your group to break into pairs or trios and pray the prayer together, reading it aloud in unison. Have them take the prayer home with them as they continue to think about the ways God desires to use them as his instrument in the context of their everyday lives. ✱

hit the road `about 5 minutes`

Pass out the "Prepared for a Purpose" handouts and pens, and then invite everyone to spread out around the room.

Say: God has been guiding you your whole life—forming you and shaping you through relationships, events, and circumstances. You may not have realized it at the time, but God has been at work. When we look back into the past, we can see the many ways God has been speaking to us, guiding us, and preparing us.

Have kids follow the instructions on the "Prepared for a Purpose" handout as they each create a time line of their lives that highlights God's work in their past.

Warn kids when there's just 1 or 2 minutes left, then have them fold up their time lines and put them in their pockets, Bibles, or journals so they can be kept private.

Wrap up with a time of prayer. Let your kids know you'll be sending **5 for 5 world tour** life

aftr u meet

Right after your meeting, send kids the first **5 for 5 world tour** challenge for them to do tomorrow via Twitter, e-mail, or by posting it on a Facebook page (or youth group Web page) you've set up. Continue to send 1 challenge each day for the 5 days following your meeting.

About 2 days after your group meets, send a text message to the kids in your small group, encouraging them to consider how they are being used as God's instruments. Prompt them to keep at it with their **5 for 5 world tour** challenges and let them know you're praying for them.

playlist

To add some ambiance to this closing self-evaluation time, download the song "Instrument of Your Peace" by the Paul Coleman Trio to your iPod (or to a CD) and play it while your jr. highers work.

5 for 5 world tour handout

application and devotional challenges for them to do each day via Twitter, e-mail, or through a Facebook group you've set up. (Or, if you prefer not to use these technology options, pass out copies of the **5 for 5 world tour** handout you've downloaded from the CD-ROM to the teens.) Encourage your kids to strive to spend about 5 minutes each day connecting with God through these devotional experiences.

9

Being Faithful for a Lifetime

The Prep

Session goal: Jr. highers will be encouraged to develop a deep-rooted faith that's characterized by daily obedience, an eternal perspective, and an enduring commitment.

Scriptures: Genesis 1:26, 27; Jeremiah 20:7-9, 14-18; Matthew 4:19; Mark 4:1-20; Acts 20:24; 2 Timothy 4:7; Hebrews 11:1; Hebrews 12:1-3

You'll need:

- Bibles
- Pens or pencils
- Paper
- Dry-erase markers
- Mirror (at least 12" by 18")
- Small plastic tablecloth
- Clay or modeling dough
- Masking tape
- Permanent markers (or ball-point pens)
- 12" by 18" cross (cut out of poster board)
- 3 dictionaries
- Piece of newsprint
- Red and black markers
- Pair of eyeglasses
- Pair of running shoes
- Plant pot
- Small plastic tub
- Potting soil
- 2 packets of seeds
- Pillows

Download and print:

- "Stations" handouts (2 of each)
- **solo/strike a chord** discussion guide (1 per teen)

Optional supplies:

✴ For **backstage pass:** CD player and CD or iPod with recommended **playlist** songs.
✴ For **hit the road:** Download and print copies of this week's **5 for 5 world tour** take-home page (1 per teen) if you are unable to use the technology options.

Setting it up:

✴ Write the word "FOOL" at the top of 1 piece of paper, the word "HERO" at the top of another, and the word "SUCCESS" at the top of another piece.
✴ Set up 5 Experience Stations as follows:

Station 1: Set out 2 copies of the handout. Also set out a mirror (at least 12" by 18") and place several dry-erase markers in front of it. In front of the mirror, place a small plastic tablecloth on the floor and set out a bunch of clay or modeling dough.

Station 2: Set out 2 copies of the handout, a 12" by 18" cross (cut out of poster board), a roll of masking tape, and permanent markers (or ballpoint pens).

Station 3: Set out 2 copies of the handout, paper, pens, and a folded paper airplane (per handout instructions).

Station 4: Set out 2 copies of the handout, several Bibles, a plastic tub filled with potting soil, and a packet of seeds.

Station 5: Set out 2 copies of the handout, pillows, paper, and pens. Also set out the 3 objects used in **encore**: a pair of eyeglasses, a pot full of soil, and a pair of running shoes.

✴ If you'd like to use the optional **playlist** recommendations, download the songs "Give Me Words to Speak" by Aaron Shust,

"Speak" by Jimmy Needham, and "Word of God Speak" by Kutless and ready your iPod or burn a CD in order to play the songs
during the session.

Leader insight:

Over the past 8 sessions you've invested prep time, prayer, and
a good deal of effort into facilitating a meaningful interaction
between your jr. highers, God, and God's Word. You've provided
spiritual moments that will serve as long-lasting memories—as
mile-markers of faith for your teens. You've enabled them to see how
God wants to use them right now, as young teenagers, to make a difference in their world. And now, in this study, you'll cast a vision for
them for the future.

In looking at Jesus' many interactions with people in Scripture, we
can get a pretty clear idea of the type of faith he desired to develop
in people...and it *definitely* wasn't an impulsive, emotion-based
faith that's little more than a flash in the pan. Jesus doesn't want
tag-alongs—he desires *followers*. In God's economy, true faith is
demonstrated in *faithfulness*. Faithfulness is expressed in 2 arenas: in
the faithfulness of daily obedience and the "cumulative" faithfulness
of an enduring commitment to Christ over days, weeks, months,
years...a lifetime.

As you've been spending time with jr. highers, you may have
noticed that they don't seem to have much of a long-term perspective
on things. In general, preteens and early teenagers have very limited
thoughts toward the future; it's pretty tough for them to imagine
themselves as an "old" adult (like you!).

But that doesn't mean they can't try! This study introduces kids
to the concept of lifelong, enduring faithfulness to Christ. With a
quick tour through Hebrews 11, your jr. highers will be encouraged to

consider how their lives will be measured. Will they be people who've obeyed God consistently, despite hardship or temptation, or will they compromise their beliefs and actions when the going gets tough?

Your kids will better connect with the idea of *daily* faithfulness—obedience in the here and now. But challenge them along both lines. How will they be faithful, all-out committed Jesus-followers today... and tomorrow... and the next day? After all, a faithful lifetime is made up of faithful *todays*.

What about you? Do you embody faithfulness to your jr. highers? Is your perspective on eternity, or is it short-sighted, easily drawn away from God's promises by the worries of today? Is your faith deep-rooted and growing, like a seed planted in good soil? Is your faith enduring, like a marathon runner who is determined to put 1 foot in front of the other all the way to the finish line? As your jr. highers will be doing during this study, be sure to also take some time yourself to reflect on the themes covered in this series and to take stock of how God has challenged you, convicted you, inspired you, and grown your faith.

As you prepare for this final session, pray: God, the artist and maker of all things, you've made me in your image. You've called me to follow you. You've gifted me to accomplish the purposes you have before me. Thank you for all that you've done in my life and in my jr. highers' lives. Show me how to be more faithful to you each and every day. Enable me to obey your will, no matter how difficult. Give me your perspective on my life and on this world. And help me to run this race set before me with perseverance and determination.

Draw my teens ever closer to you, Lord. They are in your hands. Thank you for the privilege you've given me of speaking your truth into their lives. In Jesus' name, amen.

b4 u meet

A couple of days before your group meets, send a text message to your kids reminding them of the upcoming final Speak study. Encourage them to take some time to think about all the things they've learned over the past few weeks. (If some teens don't text, send them an e-mail or a message on Facebook or MySpace.)

The Session

Rearrange or delete sections of the study to best meet your group's needs.

txt a frnd — about 5 minutes

Invite your small group to consider this question:

✦ When you die, what do you want people to say about you and the way you lived your life?

When they've got an answer, invite them to get out their cell phones and text their answer to another person in the room. (If kids don't have their own phone, they could borrow a friend's or could form pairs and talk about their answer to this question.)

When you're ready to move on to the next part of the study, have them put their cell phones away for now. ✦

mic check — about 7 minutes

Have kids form 3 groups, and give each group a marker and 1 of the papers you prepared that say *fool, hero,* and *success.* Tell kids to work together in their group to create their own definition of their word and write it on the paper. Let them know they have 90 seconds to create their definition; they should make it as close as they can to what they imagine the dictionary might say.

When time is up, have the groups exchange papers. They should read the definition written there and add anything to it that might make the definition more full or clear. Again, give them 90 seconds.

Have kids exchange papers a final time (making sure it isn't a word they've already had). Groups should read their new paper and then add a sample sentence using that word or an example of that word (as dictionaries sometimes do).

After about 90 seconds more, get everyone's attention and have each group read aloud the definition and sentence on their paper. Then pass out dictionaries and invite volunteers to read the definitions of these words in actual dictionaries. Then explain that you're going to be rethinking these concepts in your study today. Place the papers to the side to use again later. ✤

freestyle about 7 minutes

Write the word *faith* in the top left corner of a piece of newsprint. Ask kids how they would define that word. Then add the suffix *–fulness* to the end of the word to make it *faithfulness*. Ask how kids would define that word. Affirm kids' input and add your own thoughts on what the word *faithfulness* implies about long-term commitment, attention, devotion, perseverance, and attentiveness. Explain that faithfulness is a tough thing to live out. Ask:

✤ What makes it tough to be a Christian in our world?

Use a red marker to write their thoughts about what makes it difficult to be a Christian on the left side of the newsprint. (Leave blank space on the right side, because you'll add to it later.)

txt it

You may want to give your teens the option of texting their answers to you during your discussion time. Read some of their answers out loud and use them as springboards for further discussion.

Say: We all go through times of discouragement in our faith. It can be really hard to stick it out sometimes. It can be especially hard if we feel like we're doing God's will, but things aren't working out how we'd hoped. For example, we might be praying about something and feel like that prayer is never answered. Or we might get up the courage to tell a friend about Jesus, only to have that friend blow it off. It can be tough when we feel like we're failing.

Explain that we aren't the only ones who've felt this way. People in the Bible had very similar struggles. It was even tough for Jeremiah to obey God sometimes. He was persecuted, and his prophecies appeared to be "failing" because they didn't get good results. Jeremiah had a lot of hard feelings when he went through these tough times.

Invite a volunteer to read 1 of Jeremiah's complaints found in Jeremiah 20:7-9 and another volunteer to read 20:14-18.

Tell kids that despite his struggles, his apparent failures, and his sense of discouragement, Jeremiah continued to obey God. He was faithful to God's call on his life even though things didn't always turn out great for him.

Jeremiah's example shows us something really important. Faith isn't about appearing super-spiritual. It isn't about doing amazing things for God that others admire. It isn't about having great worship times or emotional highs. Ultimately it is about *faithfulness*. 🍂

solo/strike a chord handout

solo   about 5 minutes

Tell your kids you'd like them to find a spot in your meeting area where they can be alone and spend about 5 minutes reading Scripture and thinking about what it means.

Remind them that they've been learning that God wants to use them right now, as young teenagers, to make a difference in their world.

Give each teen a copy of the **solo/strike a chord** handout and a pen or pencil, inviting them to read and follow the instructions. (Have them read through only the top portion, **solo**, right now and they'll need the **strike a chord** portion in a few minutes.) Here's a copy of what they'll read:

Take 5 minutes to read Hebrews 11. Consider:
❋ What do all of these people have in common?
❋ What stands out to you most from this passage? Why?

When the kids understand what they're supposed to do, have them take off and find a spot to read and reflect. After about 5 minutes, call everybody back together. 🍂

strike a chord　about 8 minutes

Have the group now look at the bottom portion of the **solo/strike a chord** handout and use it to guide your small group Bible exploration and discussion together as a group. Here's a copy of the **strike a chord** text for you to use to guide your discussion time:

With a partner, use Hebrews 11 to answer these questions. Jot down a few answers to share with the group. Some of you might want to start in the middle of the list, or even at the end.

solo/strike a chord handout

txt it

If you want, invite kids to answer these questions both by talking aloud and by texting. As some share their answers, others can text them to you. Read some of their thoughts aloud and build upon their ideas as your group explores this topic together.

✦ Who is included in this list?
✦ Why were they included?

After giving kids a minute to jot down some notes, have them report on their discoveries. Add their thoughts to the right side of the newsprint, using a black marker this time. Feel free to condense answers, such as, "Noah: Built the ark." Don't feel like you need to write down *every* person mentioned in the passage.

Then ask:

✦ What sort of faith did these people have? How would you describe it?

✦ Why were they able to complete their difficult tasks or follow through on God's direction for them?

Affirm kids' responses and summarize their ideas. Be sure to point out that each of these people focused on the eternal promises of God and viewed those promises as greater than the temporary struggles of their lives. If teens haven't mentioned these verses yet, you may want to draw their attention to Hebrews 11:13-16 and 11:39, 40.

Say: These people were not perfect; they made mistakes, they screwed up, and they fell flat on their faces. But what this passage emphasizes for us is that these people kept going. They had a long-term perspective. ✦

encore   about 8 minutes

Read Hebrews 11:1 aloud, and say: This is true of every person listed in this chapter. They believed in God's promises even though the results of those promises were not plainly seen in this life.

Hold up a pair of eyeglasses. Say: If you wear glasses, you know how important they are. They bring things that aren't clear into focus. They give you an accurate, true perspective on the world around you.

Refer again to the reasons listed in red on the newsprint, and explain that difficult circumstances must be seen in perspective. When we focus on bleak circumstances that may be part of our life as a Christian, we become near-sighted. We don't have a full perspective because we're focusing so much on our present experience. We aren't able to fully follow Christ because of our near-sightedness. What Hebrews 11 reminds us is that no hardship is too great or so persuasive to cause us to give up our faith.

Hold up the eyeglasses and say: These glasses symbolize 1 aspect of faithfulness: having spiritual vision.

Next, hold up the pair of running shoes.

Invite a volunteer to read aloud Hebrews 12:1-3 while others follow along in their own Bibles. Say: The Apostle Paul also used the imagery of a race to describe faith in Christ.

Have volunteers read aloud Acts 20:24 and 2 Timothy 4:7.

Explain that faith involves training and hard work, just like running. The race of faith is not a sprint. It's a marathon. It's an endurance race. It's about daily faithfulness and obedience.

Now hold up the pot and seeds. Say: Jesus gives us a very powerful metaphor for faithfulness: seeds that fall on good soil, take root, and grow.

Invite volunteers to read aloud sections of Mark 4:1-20 while everyone else reads along in their own Bibles. Lead jr. highers through summarizing the parable and its meaning with some basic questions about what they observe in the passage:

✳ What was the symbolism of the first type of soil Jesus described?

(The soil on the path in 4:4 and 15)

✤ What was the symbolism of the next type of soil? (The rocky soil in 4:5, 6 and 16, 17)
✤ How about the third type? (The thorny soil in 4:7 and 18, 19)
✤ What about the fourth type of soil? (The fertile soil in 4:8 and 20)

As needed, walk kids through Jesus' explanation of the parable so they clearly understand the types of people and scenarios he is referring to. Then ask:

✤ How does this story relate to faithfulness?

Help teens zero in on the rocky soil and the thorny soil. These are both powerful pictures of the lives of people who are not faithful— people who are led away from a totally committed faith by trouble, persecution, worries, or temptation. Draw specific connections here to anything written on a newsprint sheet related to these issues.

Stick the seed down into the pot of soil, and say: Jesus' story powerfully recognizes the many things that make it tough to be a Christian in this world. He knows it isn't easy. He knows there are "rocks" and "thorns" that threaten us. And he says pretty clearly that a superficial faith won't cut it and a faith that lets temptation or hardship choke it just won't make it. (Hold up the pot.) Jesus shows us that true faith is deep-rooted and always growing. ✤

Station 1 handout

backstage pass   `about 16 minutes`

Explain to the group that they'll now take some time to journey through some experience stations. Point out where the stations are in your room.

Tell kids that they will have 15 minutes to visit the stations. They should find a partner and travel in pairs; they'll find instructions for discussion and an experience at each station.

Encourage them to take as much time as they want at each station—they don't have to make it through all of them. Also let them know that Station 5 is a spot where they can stop and take time by themselves to think or write through what God's been doing in their lives. They won't interact directly with their partner in this area. Finally, explain that they don't have to go in any order—they can visit any of the stations they'd like and in any order they want.

When everyone understands the basic idea, have kids pair up and make their way through the stations. 🌟

hit the road   `about 4 minutes`

Reiterate the key points of what you've studied and what kids have been challenged to do and consider over the past 9 weeks. Encourage your jr. highers by emphasizing God's love and grace in their lives. Then pray for your teens—pray about your vision for their lives. Pray with earnestness and passion about your desire for them to dwell in God's love and proclaim the gospel with their lives. Pray that God would give them a deep-rooted, faithful, and enduring commitment to him.

Let your kids know you'll be sending **5 for 5 world tour** life application and devotional challenges for them to do each day via Twitter,

hidden track

If you have extra time this week, give kids 20 or 25 minutes to go through the stations.

playlist

To add some powerful ambiance to this experience, download these songs to your iPod (or burn a CD) and play them (in this order) while teens move from station to station.
"Give Me Words to Speak" by Aaron Shust
"Speak" by Jimmy Needham
"Word of God Speak" by Kutless

e-mail, or through a Facebook group you've set up. (Or, if you prefer not to use these technology options, pass out copies of the **5 for 5 world tour** handout you've downloaded from the CD-ROM to the teens.) Encourage your kids to strive to spend about 5 minutes each day connecting with God through these devotional experiences.

aftr u meet

Right after your meeting, send kids the first **5 for 5 world tour** challenge for them to do tomorrow via Twitter, e-mail, or by posting it on a Facebook page (or youth group Web page) you've set up. Continue to send 1 challenge each day for the 5 days following your meeting.

About 2 days after your group meets, send a text message to your kids, encouraging them to be faithful to their commitment to Jesus. Prompt them to keep at it with their **5 for 5 world tour** challenges and let them know you're praying for them.

Scripture index